# LOVE AND REVENGE

GW00692045

## L. F. Casban

To Dame Vera Lynn
with best wishes

Leonard F. Casban

ARTHUR H. STOCKWELL LTD.
Elms Court   Ilfracombe   Devon
*Established 1898*

*All persons in this book are fictitious and are not*
*intended to represent any actual persons living or*
*dead.*

ISBN 0 7223 2763-3

*Printed in Great Britain by*
*Arthur H. Stockwell Ltd.*
*Elms Court     Ilfracombe*
*Devon*

# CONTENTS

## *PART 1*

## *PART 2*

## SUMMARY

This is a story of two girls who had one thing in common, the price of a war.

Denise Povey came from a middle-class family in Blackpool during the 1920s. She had set her sights on a dancing career, but with World War II approaching tragedy was to change her personality and revenge became the hallmark of her intentions, and so this quiet girl by nature was hardened which gave her the strength that she needed when she was also involved with murder.

But time is a healer and if your conscience is clear then you are rewarded with the fruits of life, as Denise experienced.

Wendy Dalter was also brought up in the 1920s in a working-class family who lived in Surrey. The struggle they had during those days was heading towards the same war of destruction engineered by Adolf Hitler. The part she played was one undertaken by so many of her age at that time; the disappointments that accompanied her during this period helped to mould her into a sweet reliable and trusting person who was finally rewarded, as you will see.

# INTRODUCTION

The summer holidays of 1928 brought together two schoolgirls of a similar age, whose friendship lasted forever.

One experienced love and revenge within hostile conditions; the other had love and knew what suffering really meant; but both knew the anxiety of World War II.

The troubled years of the 20s hardened these girls for the future years ahead of them.

Allow me to take you step by step through their experiences of growing up and handling the disappointments of life, as so many of us have known.

*PART 1*

## CHAPTER 1

The year is 1928, the place is Blackpool and it is August. All the children are on holiday, the sandy beaches are full of holiday-makers, the weather is hot, the sky is blue and there is a slight breeze. What more could one wish for? This was England in peacetime, and there were two young schoolgirls enjoying themselves making sand castles; but they were not sisters, in fact one girl was on holiday with her parents for two weeks and they had come from Croydon, Surrey, down the south of England. The other girl lived in Blackpool with her parents — her name was Denise Povey, and she had a sister named Mary.

The young girl from Croydon was an only child, and her name was Wendy Dalter. The two perfect strangers became everlasting friends, and on many occasions Wendy with her parents spent their summer holidays in Blackpool; and so over the many years the two girls kept up a strong friendship.

The year 1937 was a memorable year. Denise was fifteen years old, and Wendy was almost seventeen, and both girls had become attractive teenagers. Over the years since 1928, when they first met, they have understood each other and had enjoyed each other's company; but this year was the Coronation of King George VI and Queen Elizabeth, and of course all sorts of celebrations were going on everywhere.

Wendy had travelled alone to Blackpool for her annual holiday to stay at Denise's house for the last two weeks in September. They attended the occasional dance hall, and with their looks and charm they were much admired by the local lads. But for all that, romance was not top of their list.

They ate out sometimes in the local restaurants, but were always back home indoors by ten-thirty, and they dressed up for every occasion.

As the holiday came closer to the end, Wendy said "I wonder how many more holidays we will share together?"

Denise took her time to answer as they strolled along the promenade. She then looked up to the blue sky and with the warm sun pouring down she said "You know Wendy, I have been wondering about that also."

They then both stopped and leant on the promenade rail and looked out to sea where the odd boat was being tossed up and down.

Wendy took hold of Denise's hand and said "I'm afraid that Adolf Hitler means to start a war in Europe — everybody is talking about it."

"I know" answered Denise.

The two girls then went into deep thought thinking of what the future had in store for them.

It was Denise who then said "If war does come and we are involved, what do you think you will do Wendy?"

"Oh, I probably will take up nursing. I wouldn't mind looking after the wounded. I could not work in a factory. But what would you do Denise?"

"Well, I shall make use of my dancing. I shall try and get into a chorus in a London show, and if need be I would join ENSA and entertain the troops abroad — at least I might see a bit of the world?"

By this time they decided to continue their walk along the promenade.

Then Wendy said "Perhaps nothing will come of it!"

That holiday was to have been their last, because the following year 1938, Neville Chamberlain returned from Germany where Adolf Hitler signed a piece of paper in his mountain retreat, the Bergof, in Obersaltzburg, and Neville Chamberlain was seen waving the piece of paper as he walked down the steps from his aircraft saying "Peace in our time".

But it was a year of uncertainty, and holidays were not on people's minds, and as we entered 1939 it became apparent that war was inevitable, and so it was not surprising that during that year England declared war on Germany, and so both Wendy and Denise went their different ways and subsequently lost contact with each other; but sadness and sorrow, love and revenge, accompanied both girls during the coming war years. But did they ever meet again, and if they did, what stories could they tell? So let me begin with Denise Povey.

## CHAPTER 2

Denise was born in Blackpool in 1922. She also had a sister called Mary. Their mother was a local schoolteacher, and their father was a local doctor. They lived in a large detached house with a very pretty well-laid-out garden with masses of flowers and shrubs, and since it was their wish to feed the birds, it was very much like a wild aviary. It was also graced with a pond, complete with goldfish and frogs.

A very happy family life was experienced by both girls during their growing-up stages. Mary had dark hair and favoured her father in every way, so it was only natural that she eventually became a nurse. Her nature was a serious one, with her feet firmly on the ground, whereas Denise was a natural blonde with outstanding beauty, and who favoured her mother; but instead of becoming a schoolteacher she became a professional dancer, which led her to the London stage. But before reaching the heights of their careers, they both experienced the love and warmth of a happy home. Unfortunately their teenage life was during Adolf Hitler's period of power, and the time was now closing in on 1938, when Mary was eighteen years old and Denise was sixteen years old.

It was during dinner one evening that their father said "Well my dears what have you in mind to do now that war looks imminent?"

Mary was the first to answer. Without hesitation she looked across the table and directly at her father and said "I shall put all my knowledge and training into becoming a good nurse Papa."

Her father raised a smile and replied "Just as I thought dear, and a good nurse you will make I am sure."

There was silence for a few moments as Denise took another sip of wine, she then glanced down at the table. She looked towards her mother and said "I will entertain the troops with my dancing, for I know little else Papa."

The conversation continued about the dark days that lay ahead of them all, when suddenly the phone rang. Their mother answered it promptly and said "It's for you dear. I believe Mr Welbeck is not well."

Their father had a few words on the phone, and was soon on his way, which was a normal way of life to the family.

As the next day arrived, people all over England began to take Adolf Hitler seriously, and despite the piece of paper signed by Adolf Hitler regarding peace terms, no one really believed this, and so England started to prepare herself for the worst to come. Mary had passed her exams, and Denise had joined a troupe of dancers engaged in the northern music halls, of which she became a chorus girl with enormous potential.

It was 1940, at the age of eighteen, that Denise was given the chance to go to London and join a chorus. She arrived at the Stoll Theatre in the Kingsway for her first rehearsal. She was of course a little nervous but full of confidence regarding her feet. In the line, up on the stage, she met for the first time another girl who was to become her close friend. Her name being Ruth Worthy, whose home was in Coventry, and was of the same age as Denise. They passed with flying colours.

After their ordeal, they both went for refreshments in the Strand. It was Ruth who broke the ice by saying "I must admit, I was very nervous, but you were full of confidence. Have you had previous experience Denise?"

Denise answered quickly by saying "No, and I must admit I also was nervous." They both laughed and exchanged their past life. Denise then said "When we get on the road shall we share the same digs?"

"What a good idea. I would like that" said Ruth — and so a great friendship was born.

As the next few weeks went by, under the care of the Stoll Theatre, they saw for the first time life in London. As they strolled the streets during their hours of leisure, they noticed the city preparing for hard times to come now that England and Germany were at war. Sandbags were being placed around various important buildings. In Whitehall, windows had protection strips should they get broken. Gas masks were being carried by the public, and the Forces and the police were issued with helmets. The face of London had now changed overnight — the bright lights had ceased to exist — and what lay in store for both of these charming girls is about to be unfolded. The sirens were sounded as aircraft above were mistaken for enemy. This was understandable, because everyone was over cautious. This was to be the pattern of life for things to come.

It was not long before both girls were auditioned for a show to go on tour, which was a musical with well-known comedians, and it included acrobatic acts. The whole show was fast moving and very colourful. It got a very good reception at the Croydon Empire, and both girls found digs together in a boarding house in South Croydon, which was a short walk from the theatre.

After the morning rehearsal, both Denise and Ruth made their way to have lunch at the Davis Theatre Restaurant, and it was here that the future for Denise was to change. The restaurant was a very attractive one, and many tables were placed around the balcony which looked down upon the foyer, and one could observe patrons coming in. It was during their meal that they both became aware of a very good-looking young man who was staring in their direction.

It was Ruth who said "Don't look now, but I think we have attracted a very handsome young man."

Denise then said "I am aware of the fact."

"The fellow is not in a Forces' uniform, so he could be home on leave or awaiting his call-up?" was what Ruth said.

In fact his age was twenty. He had passed his medical examination and was passed grade one. What's more, he had chosen to join the RAF, and so it was only a matter of time before he would be called upon to fight for his country.

Having taken a great deal of interest in the girls he decided to walk towards their table. After he had finished his meal and paid his bill, he strolled very slowly towards their table, where he stopped and being stuck for words he said the first thing that came into his head. He stared straight at Denise then he looked at Ruth. He gave a very infectious smile and said "You both must be in show business, am I right?"

Ruth was the first to answer. "You are right so far."

This was followed by silence from all concerned then realising his embarrassing position Denise said "Was there something else?"

It was painful to watch his face as he fumbled for the right words to say, so Ruth said "If you want to see our show we are performing at the Croydon Empire."

He now felt relaxed and said "My name is Tom Blake and I live in Croydon. I will come to see your show and perhaps you will let me escort you both home tonight?" He then bade them goodbye, and without doubt, both girls took a shine to him little knowing what horror was to follow before the war was over.

That evening Tom kept his promise and went to the theatre. The show was extremely good and the talent that was put on was of high entertainment. The highlight as far as Tom was concerned were the two girls in the chorus. When the show was over and the lights came on it was not surprising how few people had attended now that the risk of being in a theatre when an air raid could occur.

Tom made his way backstage and waited for the girls — the one favoured was of course Denise. As they both came out to go home the siren was giving an alert signal for an air raid. Few people were around as all three made their way towards South Croydon. The buses had stopped and so it meant walking.

Denise said "We are both in the same digs, but have you far to go?"

"Oh no, I live not far away, please don't worry."

At that moment searchlights flashed towards the sky followed by gunfire from the ack-ack batteries. The sound of a German bomber could be clearly heard overhead, when suddenly all hell was let loose and a string of bombs came roaring down. The three of them dashed for cover into a nearby shop doorway just as the bombs exploded not far from where they were. When it was safe they left the shop doorway and continued on their way.

Soon they were at the digs and both girls thanked him for seeing them home safely.

Tom then looked at Denise and said "Would it be possible for you and me to meet during the daytime whilst the show is in Croydon?"

She replied "That would be nice."

He then said "Can I see you for lunch tomorrow at 1 o'clock in the Davis Theatre Restaurant?"

"Of course Tom. I look forward to it."

As Tom walked slowly back home, his thoughts were on two things — Denise and the war. As he entered the deserted street where he once played as a small lad, only an ARP man could be seen; then suddenly more action took place with gunfire as bombers passed overhead. He paused at the entrance of his home, then hastily he hurried through the side gate and down to the air-raid shelter where his mother and father were seeking shelter for the night.

Tom had no brothers or sisters, so he was all his parents had. His mother was a very sweet person and kind, and his father a very gentle and understanding man who was employed as an engineer in a local engineering company, now engaged on war work.

As Tom entered the air-raid shelter, which was at the bottom of the garden, his mother said "Hello son, would you like a cup of tea?"

"Oh that would be lovely Mum."

His father looked at him and said with concern "Did you enjoy the show Tom?"

With a hot cup of tea firmly gripped in his hand Tom said "Yes thanks." He then decided to tell his parents about Denise. There was of course silence in the shelter. Then Tom said "Romance is all very nice, but there is a war to be considered, and if I get my call-up papers where will it all end, and after all she is on the stage, and will she want to give up the stage after the war?"

"Well son, I cannot answer or advise you on this" said his

father — and so the conversation came to a close as they tucked down and went to sleep.

In the morning, Tom explained that he had arranged to have lunch with Denise. He worked locally in an accountancy firm, hoping one day to become a chartered accountant, but that would now have to wait until after the war when he could complete his exams. As the morning rolled on he could think only about Denise.

The time arrived for him to take lunch, so off he hurried to the restaurant, and to his amazement Denise was waiting. The day was warm and sunny, and Croydon High Street was very busy. As he approached Denise, his eyes gazed upon a beautiful young lady with her blonde hair and deep blue eyes and round face — it was like looking at Doris Day the American musical actress.

Denise had chosen to wear a very pretty flared skirt, and an attractive white blouse. She wore no stockings and was complete with a pair of cream shoes. The skirt was just below her knees and she held a shoulder-strap handbag — without doubt she was a very beautiful young lady — her smile was vivacious and the twinkle in her eyes said it all.

Tom was of course completely captivated. "Hello Denise, it's lovely to see you, and you look positively beautiful."

Her smile continued as she said "Thank you Tom, and you also look very dashing in your suit."

Their meeting started off with Cupid watching around the corner as Tom escorted Denise through the main entrance and up the stairs to the restaurant. He felt six feet tall, everybody nearby just could not take their eyes off of Denise. She was obviously in show business and Tom was so proud, after all this was the first girl he had ever dated, and as for falling in love it had never entered his head. In no time at all they had climbed the stairs and were sitting at the same table where they first met. They looked at the menu and chose the food they wanted, and a medium bottle of wine was ordered. In a way Denise knew that this was unusual for Tom to be entertaining a young lady, however he acted very attentive and she was proud to be looked after by him. He just could not take his eyes off her.

Then suddenly they both spoke at the same time. They then burst into laughter and Tom said "What were you going to say?"

"No you first please."

Tom gazed deeply into her eyes, then he held her hand across the table and said "Without doubt you are the most beautiful young lady that I have ever met. In fact you are gorgeous, and there is something else that I must tell you, I have fallen deeply in love with you."

Denise took on a serious look and said "I know how you feel because I feel the same way about you." She continued by saying something very grown-up, after all she was only eighteen years old, "We have just met. We live in two worlds, but we have one thing in common, we are involved in a war."

Tom then said "You are right. Here I am waiting for my call-up papers for the RAF, and who knows where your profession will take you, maybe even overseas on ENSA to entertain the troops?"

He released her hand and she said, "Shall we take it day by day for now?"

"That is a good idea" said Tom.

The meal was a success, after which they left the restaurant, he returned to his office and she wandered around the town looking at the local stores.

After work he returned home and explained to his mother what had taken place over lunch.

His mother said "If it's possible we must meet this young lady?"

"Of course Mum. I would like that."

Soon it was time for Tom to go to the theatre and meet Denise after the show. All was quiet that evening, for there were no sirens. So the walk home to her digs was a romantic one, and on the doorstep of the boarding house Tom made the approach to hold her in his arms for the first time, and in doing so he experienced a pain that he had never had before. As their bodies became one and their lips met with passion, the kiss seemed timeless. Their eyes were closed and the thought of war was miles from their inner thoughts. Then came the moment of relaxation as Tom released his hold and opened his eyes. Denise's were still closed. He just could not resist another kiss. The whole thing emotionally was harmless — it was an embrace of true love and respect. Not a word was spoken. Tears almost entered Tom's eyes as he realised all this was on borrowed time, but it was to be his greatest moment in his life and one that he will always remember to his dying day. What lay ahead, only the powers above knew this.

They both gave out a sigh and Denise said "Thanks Tom for everything."

"No thank you Denise for coming into my life when I needed you most."

As he walked on his way home, he was walking on air, and in no time at all he was back home and explaining his feelings to both his parents.

As the week rolled on, and a repeat of meetings occurred, he found himself truly in love. But when Friday morning arrived with the post informing him of his call-up to report at Uxbridge, it was to be the beginning of his RAF career.

That evening was a very sad one for Denise and Tom, and it was after her show that they strolled through the local park called Park Hill. Again there was no air raid. As they passed the flowerbeds arm in arm, they found and sat down upon a park seat. Deep thought was on their minds as they held hands.

Denise was the first to break the silence by saying, "Tom, I truly love you with all my heart, but Sunday I have to return home to Blackpool as the show finishes here. But I return to London in a week's time for rehearsals of a new show which I think will be in Brighton."

It was then that Tom said "I have to report to Uxbridge next Monday for details of my training and posting."

They then both got up and strolled in the darkness out of the park and along High Street towards South Croydon. On their arrival once again at Denise's digs, they embraced each other for what seemed endless.

"I will come along and meet you here tomorrow at 9 o'clock and spend the whole day with you darling. I will also come to the show and see you home" said Tom.

"Thank you Tom."

They were both obviously in love.

On his way home there were very few people around, but again there were no German bombers, so a peaceful stroll home was experienced, and he was in deep thought as to what the future held in store for himself and Denise; but in those days of difficult times, one always thought the worst.

The next day started cloudless with blue skies. The sun was already getting warm. So up with the lark, and a hug for his mum, Tom set off to meet the girl of his dreams. Denise was waiting when he arrived, and for the first time he met the boarding house landlady. She was not very tall, but very charming. She explained how she had enjoyed having both girls stay in her house. Ruth also came to the front door and said "See you later."

They then both went on their way to a local coffee house near West Croydon Station.

It was during this interlude that Tom said "I know it's early days, and we have no idea what the future holds for us, but I would love to buy you an engagement ring. It will be a bond for whatever may happen. What do you say darling?"

With her bright blue eyes she said "I would be proud to wear it and let our destiny decide our future."

So out of the cafe they strolled, along the busy Croydon High Street.

Their next stop was of course the jeweller's. Without hesitation they both walked inside and Tom said to the shop assistant "May we see your selection of engagement rings?"

A tray was produced and one ring stood out amongst them all — a truly beautiful diamond saphire set in platinum and gold. The fit was perfect. The price mattered not.

After much excitement, the assistant said "Congratulations to you both. You make a charming couple."

The next stop was East Croydon Station, where they boarded a train for Victoria Station. The whole journey was one of love and joy. On their arrival, they left the station and made their way up Victoria Street where Tom purchased a rose and fixed it to Denise's lapel of her fitted jacket of her navy-blue suit. She wore a white blouse and matching dark blue court shoes. She was also carrying a handbag. She looked really beautiful and Tom was so happy as they walked past Westminster Abbey and into Whitehall. The atmosphere was a little solemn, what with the sandbags everywhere. Nevertheless they arrived at Trafalgar Square where they passed Nelson's Column and nurse Edith Cavell's Statue. They continued into Charing Cross Road, and cut through to Leicester Square. It was now lunch time, so Tom suggested they eat at the Swiss Restaurant. Denise was so thrilled to be holding Tom's arm.

What one has to remember, is that Tom seldom went to London, and so all this was new to him, but he was so happy that he took it all in his stride as though he had done all this before. It was all due to the fact that he had such an outstanding beauty on his arm.

"Oh Tom this is wonderful," said Denise.

"Yes darling, you are so right."

After a great lunch, they strolled up Piccadilly and entered several shops, where they purchased the odd gift for Denise to celebrate their engagement — such as a beautiful scarf, and a delicate gold watch. Soon they were passing the Ritz Hotel. They stopped and looked in the doorway.

Denise said "When the war is over, this is where we will hold our wedding reception."

"What a wonderful thought, and to think it may come true" said Tom.

They then entered Green Park, and with the sun shining and a few people sitting on the grass and the odd person taking their dog for a walk, the atmosphere was so great it was difficult to imagine that there was a war with Germany.

They sat on a park seat. When an old Chelsea pensioner strolled by, getting support from his walking stick, he was kind enough to smile and say "You're the right age for love, but it's the wrong period, so do be careful, and I wish you both all the happiness I can see shown in your faces."

Tom said "What a wonderful old man. He obviously has seen many difficult and hard times."

"I agree dear" said Denise.

It was not long before they started on their way through the park, and occasionally ducking under the trees that hung low in the park. As they strolled along the pathway, they took note of the children enjoying themselves. What lay ahead for these happy folk no one could forecast, and the tragedy that awaited for Tom and Denise, no one could have possibly predicted.

Their walk was nearly over as they strolled down Birdcage Walk, passing by the walled grounds of Buckingham Palace, when suddenly in front of them came Victoria Station, where they sat and had a cup of tea in the platform cafe. The time now was 4 p.m., and the train they had to catch was at 4.20 p.m., so with their return tickets they were soon passing through the platform gate and onto the train.

The journey was taken up by talking about their wonderful London trip, and of course of their love for each other. Cupid's arrow had really struck home with Tom and Denise.

As they arrived back at East Croydon Station, once off the train, they made their way down George Street and on to her digs.

This day will remain in both of their hearts to the day they die, that I can assure you. All that remains is for Tom to see the evening show for the last time, and to see his sweetheart back to her digs, for tomorrow was Sunday, and Tom had to see Denise up to London where she would catch her train for the North.

It was now Sunday, and Tom made his way to meet Denise and take her to London where she would catch her train and return home to Blackpool. Arm in arm they left her digs and made their way to East Croydon Station. They had little to say to each other except that they held onto each other tightly as they walked finally into the station entrance, where Tom purchased two tickets to London — but one was a single ticket. They slowly walked down the slope to the platform and waited for the train to arrive.

It was Tom who said "Now remember darling, I will phone you tonight, so do take care dear."

Denise looked at him and said "Yes I will Tom, and you also must be careful."

The train pulled into the station and they both got in quickly. Once they were seated, their hands were clasped tightly. They talked about their first meeting and of all the happy moments they had spent together. Denise fingered and admired her engagement ring. They also noticed all the bomb damage that had been done, which became a reminder of the dangers that lay ahead of them.

In no time at all the train was pulling into the station platform. They both stepped from the train and made their way through the departure gate and into the station cafe. The station was very busy, so it helped to take their minds off of the sad departure. Inside the cafe, they spent their last few precious moments together over a cup of tea, before Denise continued to travel up North on her own.

This was the scene of unhappiness as their eyes looked at each other and said it all. Somehow they both got the idea that all was over. Whatever gives one this knowledge, you can never tell. Is it because such happiness never lasts, or in their case was it because of the old Chelsea pensioner's remark, or just because it was in troubled times, with such an uncertain future? After all, Adolf Hitler was confident of winning.

Soon it was time for them to leave the cafe and say their goodbyes. They embraced quietly and held onto each other firmly.

Then Denise said "Take care Tom. I love you so very much. I will write and let you know what I am doing."

They then kissed and kissed again. They then stood just holding hands and Tom said "Remember I will love you until I die, and thanks for coming my way."

Their hands then slipped apart as Denise walked away. She had the strangest feeling that she would never see Tom again. She then stopped and turned around to look in Tom's direction. The sun shone down through the station glass roof onto Tom. She waved, and he also waved back. Then suddenly the sun was so bright that Tom disappeared as though he was a ghost. She hesitated and wanted to turn back, but somehow when she looked again, Tom was not there.

Tom had walked away to catch his train back to Croydon. During the journey he had thoughts only of Denise, and he too wondered was that to be the last time that they will ever see each other. Tears slowly came from his eyes as the motion of the train lulled him into romantic thoughts, and of the only girl that he had ever fallen in love with.

When he arrived home, his parents could see all too clearly how upset he was. They tried making polite conversation, but it was all in vain. When he finally went to bed, he cried himself to sleep.

# CHAPTER 3

It was now Monday morning and Tom was on his way to Uxbridge on more serious business. When he arrived, he was not alone, for there were many such young men being called upon to do their duty. After the preliminary discussions of what is expected of him and to the type of training required for aircrew duties, Tom soon settled down to a new way of life, and was soon thrown into training for a navigator and wireless operator. The training was strict and the demand for such persons was top priority, and in no time at all he was ready for operational flying. But before joining an operational squadron, he was granted leave after which he had to report to Scampton.

It all seemed that he had grown up too quickly, but at least he had a lot in common with his fellow mates, for their way of life was all new to what they had been used to; but they had comradeship as never before experienced — they all needed each other, and team work was very important.

Tom soon settled down at Scampton and it was not long before he was on his first mission, Düsseldorf, which was well protected with balloons and ack-ack batteries; and then came Darmstadt. But after several months of extensive operations he was set for Essen which was the home of Krupps and his industries. Such targets were heavily fortified, and so on such missions, heavy losses were experienced.

Whilst all this was going on, Denise had completed several tours in many big cities, and had applied to join ENSA, and her first trip to entertain the troops was India.

By the time Tom had been home on leave and seen all the

suffering that London and its suburbs were experiencing through the heavy bombing, he returned to his base feeling rather sad — at least he now had several letters to read from Denise.

It was during the bombing of Hamburg when things did not go too well. The city was ablaze and the ack-ack batteries were firing constantly. The searchlights picked out many bombers just as Tom's bomber had unloaded their bombs. Their plane was hit and one engine was on fire. The plane started to lose height. Then the plane was hit again and it was decided that they should all bale out as quickly as possible. Tom landed safely, but was quickly captured and so became a prisoner of war. After being interrogated, he was sent to a prison not far from Munich. He was of course well treated to start with, but after a few days he was transferred to a prison near Würzburg. The commandant was a Heidrick Von Steinrickter. He was a very ruthless man with a hatred for the English, and a strong Nazi believer.

For some reason or other, he seemed to pick on Tom, and interrogated him regarding the strength of the RAF, and to where was his base in England. Such information Tom was not in a position to reveal, but the commandant refused to believe Tom and so ordered him to be tortured. The pressure that was put on Tom was truly terrible. However, a strange thing happened, one of the prison guards fell ill with violent stomach pains and a soldier from the regiment took his place — it was whilst what little food was given to Tom. This soldier knew very little of prison procedure and so Tom decided to take advantage of the situation. But further luck came Tom's way, for when he took a closer look at the soldier, he was Tom's double. Tom decided to scream in pain as though he needed to use the toilet. The soldier being a novice helped Tom to the toilet quarters. Tom took full advantage of this soldier's weakness, and he struck the soldier hard on the neck whereby knocking him out. He promptly changed his prisoner of war dress with the soldier, and put the German soldier back in his cell. From here on it was easy except the risk Tom took was, would he be found out by other soldiers? This was the risk that he gambled on, after all, he knew that with further torture he would die, so what had he to lose!

Tom could speak a little German and what he knew he spoke well, and now that he was the guard on duty he was in control to seeing that the German made no other contact to explain what had happened. When the prison officer returned to his job, Tom rejoined his unit. He complained of stomach pains and so he was relieved of duty; but how long would this all last? Somehow Tom knew that he had to make his escape. His position was very delicate to say the least of it. Apparently, the German that Tom swopped places with failed to convince Von Steinrickter of what had happened, and since he also could not furnish him with the information he needed, he had him shot. This left Tom completely in the clear.

As the weeks went by, Tom failed to find a way to escape; but just by chance, Tom's destiny altered. The regiment was ordered to Greece, and Tom thought that if he could now get onto allied soil, there was a chance. The regiment was ordered to Athens and the commander unfortunately was of course Heidrick Von Steinrickter. As the battalion moved into Athens, they were stationed in Ammonia Square.

As the following weeks went by, Tom experienced a rather relaxing time. He visited the Acropolis and also the old part of Athens, and it was during one of these relaxed moments that he visited a certain restaurant where he overheard a Greek talking to another Greek about information recently received by radio of military movements. Tom realised that these Greeks were involved with the Greek resistance. Very discretely Tom spoke to one of them in English and in what little Greek he knew. First of all they doubted his good intentions and they took no notice of him, but one Greek named Spiros had an English friend in the resistance that had been flown in from England some weeks before. The Englishman agreed to meet up with Tom to try and see if he really was English, and could he be of use to the movement.

Tom returned that evening after getting permission to leave the barracks. His movements did not arouse any suspicion as many of the soldiers were able to get such freedom.

Whilst he sat at the table on his own, still dressed in his army uniform, so as not to arouse anything suspicious, suddenly a very attractive Greecian girl walked towards his table and paid the attention to a soldier, as was so often done. She sat down. Tom wondered at first was this wise to encourage such a girl when he had something special to do?

However, she said in Greek 'Cala spara' which means good evening.

Tom understood this and he encouraged her to speak Greek.

"You are alone?" she said.

Tom answered "Yes."

His Greek was very good and so she said "You speak very good Greek for a German."

This was difficult to answer, but he said "Tell me are you looking for company?"

It was obvious that she was cautious and Tom could see this.

"It depends on who you are" she said.

Tom's eyes moved around the cafe, but nothing else helped him in wondering just what to do. He then asked her "Would you like a drink?"

Her eyes were dark brown and she wore a very flimsy colourful frock. She also had very attractive bracelets on her arms, and her hair was black, long and very soft. She said "My name is Zoi. What is yours?"

At this point he felt he could take chances and said "Tom".

Her reaction was swift, she then said "Would you like to come to my flat, it is just down the road?"

He accepted and they both promptly got up and strolled out of the cafe and along the road.

Within minutes she stopped and walked through an open door where there was a staircase to various flats on various floors. On the second floor, they walked along a narrow passage and then stopped. She took out her key and in they went.

Silence was experienced as she said "Please do sit down."

Within moments two men appeared. Tom looked at both of them. They also sat down. Then one of them spoke in German very quickly and it was obvious that Tom did not understand a word he was saying. Then within a few moments the man clearly spoke in English.

Tom gave a sigh of relief and said "Thank God you are English."

"That's right old boy, and so are you. What I want is you to tell me all about yourself and how you became a German soldier. We have some knowledge about you, but we must be sure."

Tom now relaxed and explained everything to their satisfaction, and so it was agreed that Tom could be their informer regarding German military movements. They agreed to a meeting place and to a code name so that messages could be passed on quickly. As it was, Tom was able to give them some valuable information there and then. Tom's knowledge of radio equipment came in handy.

When Tom returned back at the base, he was asked to join the RT operations. Although this gave him the valuable opportunity of transmitting information without being suspected, he had to be very careful that other station operators did not become aware of secret information leaking out.

For some while, everything was just fine, and Tom's duties kept him away from getting too involved with other Germans. As the months went by, the German high command suspected something was going on because the Allied troops always seemed to anticipate the Germans' movements. This was brought to the commandant's attention, who was of course Heidrick Von Steinrickter, who was of a suspicious nature, and it was unfortunately during one of his inspections that he walked into the wireless operating room and looked carefully at all the staff. His eyes focussed on each and everyone of them and he held a conversation with everyone. When he approached Tom, he was engaged on a military call which meant that the commandant could not talk with him, but he stared very hard at Tom because when on duty and using the apparatus Tom was not wearing a hat. So the commandant walked from side to side of Tom as though he thought he recognised him, but what puzzled the commandant was why should he think he knew Tom, which was unlikely because of Tom being of such a lower rank. The commandant never mixed with the lower classes. However he then walked away, but at the door he paused, shook his head then continued on his way. As he walked to his staff car, the conversation he had with other officers took his mind off of Tom.

It was about two weeks later, when over dinner with several high ranking officers, that the conversation got onto villainous subjects such as torturing prisoners of war for information, and one officer said "No one tortures prisoners more than Heidrick. Is that so Heidrick?"

"Oh I don't know" said Heidrick. Then he said "But I must admit, I do enjoy it." He then put his glass of wine to his lips and said "To torture."

They all did likewise and then another officer said "Can you remember the last one you tortured Heidrick?"

They all laughed and sang the SS song, but the face of Heidrick looked very serious and an officer said "Well Heidrick, why the serious look? Do you really remember the last one?"

Heidrick stood up and stepped back from the table and with his glass in his hand he said "Yes I do. I thought I had recognised his face. I am sure I am right."

They all looked astonished and one officer said "What's it all about my friend?"

"Tomorrow you will know what it's all about."

It was getting late and Heidrick did like his beauty sleep.

First thing in the morning Heidrick had an officer go to the wireless operating room and bring Tom, who was on duty, to his office.

Upon entering the commandant's office he said "Sit down we must have a little talk." The only other man present was a non-commissioned officer. Heidrick looked straight at Tom and said "Tell me about yourself. Where were you born? Your military training, and where were you stationed before this posting?"

Tom tried hard to answer his questions, but he knew that

this man had recognised him, when suddenly Heidrick stood up from his desk, he thumped the table very hard. Then he walked closer to Tom and grabbed Tom's hair and pulled his head sharply backwards and said "You took a German's uniform from a man you beat up and put him in your place, and so you had me kill him instead of you. Don't deny it. You leave me with no alternative but to torture you because not only of what you did, but you are the informer giving valuable information to the Greek resistance movement. Is that not so?"

Tom did not answer straight away, but then said "If you torture me and kill me you will be killing yet another German, and if I am what you say then you will face trial after the war regarding the Geneva Convention."

"Silence dog" said Heidrick as he punched Tom in the face. He then ordered the soldier present to take Tom and clap him in irons.

Tom's hopes of surviving the war now looked hopeless as he was thrown into a cell. The conditions in the cell were terrible, and after several days he was taken into a room which consisted of only a table and one chair. Within moments two men in civilian clothes entered and introduced themselves as Gestapo staff. With Tom now sitting down they questioned him about the Greek resistance and promised him that if he collaborated he would not be punished and would go free in order to assist them with information of the resistance. The choice was his. He knew that if he helped them, innocent people would die and be tortured, so he decided to do the honourable thing and remain silent.

The two men then left the room and Tom was taken back to his cell.

A few days later the procedure was repeated, but Tom remained silent. Within the next day Tom was taken to a torture chamber where he was handcuffed to a wall and his shirt ripped from his body. Then with chains he was slashed repeatedly until he fainted. He was left all night in a chained position; and the next day without food or water, the thrashing was repeated, and Tom collapsed again.

After several days of this treatment, finally Heidrick himself entered the torture chamber and ordered unbelievable torture. Tom's hands were finally smashed, his legs torn from underneath him; but this time Tom was dead. They left Tom in this condition and locked the door.

Tom's last information he gave to the resistance enabled the Allied forces to gain ground which would have taken not only more lives but months, whereas with such information the Allies advanced in days, and the Germans were on the retreat and they were hoping to leave Greece and get to Italy.

# CHAPTER 4

Whilst all this was going on, Denise had returned from her ENSA tour in India only to find out what terrible things had happened to Tom, who was found in the cell just as Heidrick had left him when the Allies advanced through Greece, pushing the German Army out towards Italy.

Denise, now in London, met up with Ruth. They were preparing for a show in London. As they were sitting in Lyons Corner House tearooms, Denise said "What I want to do Ruth, is to join the SOE and go to Greece where our troops are fighting the German Army."

Dear Ruth could not believe what she was hearing and said "But that is very dangerous Denise. What do you want to do that for?"

Denise answered quickly and said "I want to help the Greek resistance and maybe find this Heidrick and kill him."

The very thought of all this frightened Ruth because it was out of character of Denise — she was not a violent girl and had no knowledge of such work, but as Denise said "Surely I can be trained, and if I am sent to Greece I have one thing in my favour."

"And what is that?" said Ruth.

"Well, an aunt of mine married a Greek who owned a restaurant in Blackpool, and so Greek was often spoken when I was little, and so I can speak very good Greek."

Ruth looked straight at Denise and said "Well what can I say. You look very determined I must say, but tell me are you going to do all this just to get revenge on a German?"

Denise looked up from the table and said "Well yes."

Ruth took another look at Denise and said "Now what happens if you do succeed in making the grade and you are sent to Greece, and by this time the German responsible for Tom's death has been drafted back to Germany, then what?"

Denise sighed and said "Look Ruth, I intend to try, and what's more, at least I can be of better use helping the resistance out there than just entertaining folk back home."

Ruth was a little cross when she said "Oh thanks if that's all you think I am capable of doing."

"I did not mean that, and you know it," said Denise.

"I know dear and I should not have said that."

They completed their light lunch and then strolled out of the cafe and walked into the Strand. They looked into many shops and enjoyed being together.

It was during their walk down Whitehall that Denise decided to pop into one of the ministerial offices which was closely guarded. When she stated what she wanted, she was allowed to go inside. Her object was to ask about the SOE. The young lady who attended to her, used a great deal of caution, but she did advise Denise of which office where she should make her enquiries.

She then rejoined Ruth and said "I know where to go." But as it was of no interest to Ruth, they decided to meet up later.

Denise was if course a little bit nervous, but her ultimate aim was so strong that she overcame this side of her character. She entered the building which was very confusing. She did eventually enter an office where she was asked to take a seat. The waiting time seemed endless and about half an hour later a tall very distinguished gentleman, dressed not in uniform, sat opposite her at the table and said "Now my dear what is it you want to know and how can I be of assistance to you?"

Denise felt very strong because she had been made to wait such a long time. Then she said "I am wanting to know how I can join and be of assistance to the SOE?"

"That's it is it?" said the gentleman. He then carried on by saying, "We will get to know all about you of course, but briefly I would like you to tell me why you feel this need to join such a selective movement, and what made you feel this way, and above all please tell me something about yourself — please take your time?''

Denise then explained her background such as where she was born, her dancing career, what she has been doing for ENSA.

He interrupted her and said "That's all very interesting. We will of course check out all of what you tell me, but there is more to it than that I am sure?''

She then looked him straight in the eye and explained everything about Tom.

He then said "You know there is more to being in this department than just revenge. For instance you mentioned Greece, do you speak Greek?''

"Yes'' was her firm reply.

"Have you ever been to Greece?''

"Yes'' was her second reply.

"How do you think you will react to the tough and strict training in order to make you strong enough to become a member of the SOE?''

She then said "With my determination I will overcome any ordeal that you will put me through.''

He then asked her "Would you like to join me with a cup of tea?''

"Yes please!''

He then picked up the internal phone and requested tea and biscuits. By the time the tray of tea arrived, he was impressed by Denise and of her intentions. He then said "You take sugar?''

"No thank you'' she answered.

"Well Miss Povey, you realise we shall have to have further meetings, but I can tell you this, you are a person, if satisfactorily trained, could be useful to our organisation and therefore we will be in touch very quickly, in fact within the next few days so, will we be able to contact you this quickly?''

"Oh yes'' said Denise.

And so after a few preliminary details, she left the office building feeling very proud and excited of the prospects of joining such an organisation and being given the chance to do something for her country, and who knows may also receive after the war some order of merit, plus the fact that she could have revenge on an undesirable character as Heidrick Von Steinrickter.

As planned she met up with Ruth, and as they quietly entered a cafe and sat down for a cup of tea she told Ruth "All I can say it will be possible for me to join you know what, but I can say no more. For this I am pleased, but I wish I could tell you more my dear friend."

Ruth did not press her for more information but she did say "I am pleased Denise, but do be very careful, and I wish you luck my dear."

The day ended by the two girls returning to their shared digs in Charing Cross Road. The following day they both had to attend the office of their agent who informed them that rehearsals for a new show were to begin in one week's time. It was now time for them to relax in the big city. Denise and Ruth phoned their parents, but Denise only talked about the show.

It was three days later that Denise received a phone call requesting her to attend another interview. This time it was in an old large house in Stockwell.

Denise was up early and made her way to the address given. It was on the main road and so she was able to get off the bus almost outside the building. It was a detached building built before the turn of the century. She walked through the garden entrance which once had wrought iron gates, but they had been removed for making arms. She strolled down a long gravel path towards the steps leading up to the front door which had tall columns; it was a typical house built in the period of the horse-drawn carriage. Once up the steps, she rang the bell. In no time at all the large door opened and she was greeted with a smile by an elderly lady, smartly dressed. "Come in Miss Povey. Please do go up the stairs." Upon arrival on the first floor, the lady opened the door and said "Miss Povey, Major."

The door was then closed and he asked her to be seated. "Did you have any difficulty in finding us Miss Povey?"

"Not at all," was her sharp reply.

"Then I will come straight to the point" he said as he

stared straight at her. He then said "We have done our homework on you, and so far we are satisfied with our findings, but we must stress the secrecy of these interviews. The contents of our conversations, must go no further than between you and me, which is for your safety as well as our operation's — the first thing is total silence and trust. We are very professional and have vast experience in operating such dangerous missions, but this I will tell you, we would not engage you on anything that we suspect that you could not handle. Always remember this, and whilst you are engaged on any mission we are with you all the way, but should you get caught then you will be truly on your own and the outcome of whatever happens to you will be on your own head. It will pay you to clearly understand this right now. Is that clear Miss Povey?"

Denise realised the seriousness of what she was undertaking and so she answered without hesitation "I understand perfectly."

The major looked straight at Denise and said "Very well my dear, I think we are going to get on very nicely." As he continued to outline various aspects of the job, he did mention that it is possible that they may never meet again, and so the next interview would no doubt be with another gentleman, and another destination.

Denise was impressed with what she could be called upon to do, and to think that the job would give her the opportunity of giving her the revenge she wanted — but as the gentleman said "Don't let your personal desires cloud your better judgement."

Denise had a smile on her face as she looked at the major and said "I will not put other people's lives in danger for my own personal desires."

He looked at her and said "This I believe, and it is because of this I think you are worth the risk."

It was soon after this conversation that their meeting came to an end and he said "Please be patient. We will be in touch and it will come sooner than you think."

A further week passed and another meeting took place in Kensington with yet another Army officer, who closed the interview by giving Denise instructions as to where she was to start her training.

Denise returned to her home in Blackpool before finally starting her military training. It all looked strange to her as she walked down the road where she had spent all her childhood days, and as she opened the door of her house all was quiet. She then opened the lounge door and there peacefully her mother was sitting on the settee. She turned her head and jumped up throwing her arms around Denise. The embrace was endless then her mother said "I will make a cup of tea."

Denise went into the kitchen and put her arms around her mother and said "Mum, I am shortly going on my training for special duties, and you must not worry about me. I will not be allowed to discuss my movements, and our correspondence between each other must go through a certain channel in London."

Her mother turned away, from the sink and said "What does that mean?"

"It means Mum that your letters and mine will be censored and you will not know where I am at all times, so please do not worry if anything was to go wrong. You will be the first to know this I can promise you, but all this is for my safety."

Her mother seemed to be more relaxed because of the way that Denise had explained everything. Denise also felt happier now that her mother was aware of her commitments and was of course a person to be trusted, especially as it was for her daughter's safety, which depended on her silence.

Denise then said "Should anyone ask about me Mum, just say that I am still on the road in show business."

"I understand dear" said her mother.

The next few days passed very quietly, but then came the dreaded day when Denise had to say goodbye to her parents and sister Mary. They all stood on the railway platform waiting for the train that was to separate them for how long no one knew. When suddenly the train arrived, they embraced each other and shared their kisses. They said goodbye, which was going on everywhere, with people sharing their last moments — it was a way of life — the thoughts were — when will it all end?

The train pulled out of the station leaving them all waving frantically and Denise hanging out of the window, until she and the train faded away in the distance. Denise sat down and looked out of the window as she had done so many times in the past, but that was when she was going on tour. This of course was much different and much more serious. As the miles came between her and Blackpool her heart sank a little. She did not doubt that what she was about to do was a mistake. Far from it, all she was concerned about was how good could she do the job and will she also have revenge on a monster who should not be allowed to live and continue his violent atrocities? This gave her strength, and she saw herself for the first time not only as a very beautiful girl, but her beauty could be her passport to a successful career. She was by now well on her way to the destination where her training was to begin. Several times she closed her eyes and buried herself in her thoughts.

The end of the journey came in sight. She was met at the station by a woman who introduced herself as only Denise would understand. The pair of them went to an awaiting car parked outside the station entrance. A very friendly conversation was struck up with this lady who put Denise at ease immediately — a little laughter was exchanged between them both. The lady was a lot older than Denise. She had dark brown hair, with brown eyes; very little make-up on, and wore a two-piece suit; the heels of her court shoes were not high.

It was in no time at all that the car was driving through a large wrought iron gate, and finally coming to a halt outside a very large house, which had columns at its entrance. They both entered through a large door which was attended by a male civilian who invited them inside to the main hall. After a few words, Denise was shown to her quarters.

Clutching her small suitcase, she walked up a large ornate iron staircase, then along a corridor and into a very nice bedroom. She looked around just as the lady said to her "Make yourself at home my dear. You will meet others shortly before dinner." The door then closed and Denise was alone once again. She put her case on the floor close to her bed, then she walked over to the window.

The window was draped with heavy curtains. The house obviously belonged to a wealthy person who had no doubt given it to the department for training the SOE unit. When looking through the window, she gazed upon a well-laid-out garden with conifers, and pathways lined with roses; it was a typical country home of some nobleman.

After putting what few clothes she had in the wardrobe, she sat on the side of the bed in deep thought.

Soon the silence was broken by the door opening and a voice said "Will you come this way please."

Promptly Denise followed the young lady downstairs and into a large room where many other males and females were waiting to greet her. In no time at all the preliminary introductions were over and Denise realised that they were to be her companions during her training period. They were of course of all various ages, but all very mature. The men and the women were all aware of what was expected of them. The team was now complete. All that remained was the training.

Within moments, the chatter was broken up by the knowledge that dinner was being served. So into the dining room they all strolled and each picked their own seat. As they sat down the conversation among them all was of a very relaxed and cheerful nature.

After dinner they all strolled into the music room where plenty of chairs were available, and so the intimate chatter continued. They discussed their way of life and of their feelings towards the job that they had all taken to do. When the time came to retire and go to bed, after a cup of coffee, Denise walked into her bedroom undressed, climbed into bed and fell fast asleep very quickly, as she had had a very busy day.

The morning arrived too quickly, and soon Denise was having breakfast with everyone else. She felt a little tense now, because this was the day that her training began, and so after breakfast she and the others made their way to a room laid out like a classroom, and there on the platform stood the instructor who was an army major. His age was around fifty-five — a very serious type of person, whose eyes were upon everybody in that classroom. His voice was loud, firm and clear. His first remark was "Let me introduce myself. My name is Major Colt-Brown. I am here to give you all instructions on the exams and training that you will receive over the next few weeks, and if at any time you do not understand what I am saying, please speak up instantly as we have not a moment to lose. Our services are required urgently. What I can tell you right now, is that we have many agents operating in enemy-occupied countries, and they need help and it's up to us to give them this help. So I would appreciate your complete and utter attention at all times. Have I made myself clear?"

This opening speech was met with silence, but with attention.

Denise soon settled down to the programme laid out. She was as a young girl a very studious type when it came to exams, but regarding the physical courses that lay ahead she felt she could handle this because of her determination in settling an old score. Her beauty of course was to be an added advantage to the success of what lay ahead of her.

As the weeks passed, she learned to understand the seriousness of her job.

When the courses came to an end, she once more had a spot of leave and so she returned home to Blackpool and took advantage of spending every moment with her mother. They went shopping together. They walked along the promenade. They took morning coffee and afternoon tea. Denise wondered what the future held for her in the dangerous job that she had been now trained to do.

However the day arrived when once again goodbyes were exchanged on the station platform. With tears now in everybody's eyes, the thoughts were of one, and as her father held her in his arms he said "Do be careful darling. I know the price you may have to pay, but come home please."

It was now her mother's turn to embrace. Words could not express her mother's feelings as tears poured down her face but she did say "God will walk with you, I know this darling, believe me."

And now it was her sister who had taken time off to say goodbye. They held each other tightly and Mary said "Bye bye for now. See you soon. I'll be thinking of you everyday."

They then kissed just as the train was pulling into the station.

The journey to London was a sad one for Denise, but during the journey a young airman got into conversation with her. The train was packed, the corridor was full of people standing — mostly dressed in military uniforms — but there were a few civilians. It was now getting dark and the compartments had their blinds drawn. When the train pulled into a station you had to know if it was your station because all station nameplates had been removed in order to make it difficult for any undesirable informers. It was now a way of life under wartime conditions. The airman was still holding a friendly conversation with Denise. She thought he was hoping for a date, but she was being very careful not to get involved.

The train arrived in London and the passengers started to get off. The young airman said "Can I at least treat you to a bite to eat, and maybe see you home?"

With a charming smile on her face Denise said "That is very kind of you, but no thank you." And so through the ticket barrier they walked and Denise said "I wish you luck, goodbye."

The fellow looked disappointed, but that is how it had to be for Denise in the future.

London now, and the suburbs, were being bombed every night, and that also became a way of life. You finished work and then made your way home to an air-raid shelter. It was now the month of May 1944, and a lot of action was going on in Greece. The outlook looked good for the Allies — they were beginning to worry the Germans.

Denise was summoned to the SOE headquarters where she met a high-ranking military gentlemen who discussed the requirements of her services and of the danger that she would experience. She was calm and attentive — their eyes seldom left each other during the conversation.

Then finally he shook her hand and said "Well my dear,

you have two problems. One is to carry out your mission successfully, and the other is that you are very beautiful, so use your beauty wisely, and it could be your best asset. Don't drop your guard for a moment.''

He finished with a smile and she said ''I will use my skills one hundred per cent, and my beauty will be to the enemy's disadvantage.''

''I know what you mean. While he is admiring your body, he will not notice the dagger in your hand, but be wise and take care, good luck and come home.''

# CHAPTER 5

Denise's training included parachute jumping, and for this she showed no fear. Within a couple of days she was taken to an RAF base. She was briefed, and well looked after. The following day she was made ready for her destination, which was to fly into Cyprus, where in Nicosia, arrangements would be made for her to be dropped somewhere in Greece. The whole operation went off smoothly and in no time at all Denise was among friends, eating drinking and discussing her next move.

Within a couple of days she was on her final journey, which was to be in enemy-occupied territory, and the dropping point was near Pirgos, a small coastline town on the west side of Greece. Denise was a little bit familiar with this part of Greece, only because before the war as a schoolgirl she had a holiday with her parents on the Island of Zakinthos.

Late at night she was dropped in a wooded area close to Pirgos. Within minutes, after disposing of her chute, she was met by the Greek resistance and was hurriedly taken to a nearby villa where she was briefed and given something to eat. She felt comfortable with the Greeks.

The one in charge said "It is good to have you and I understand you can operate this equipment?" which he showed her.

"No problem Nicol" she said. She then looked around the room and smiled at all the other members of the resistance. She then said "It is such a shame that I am here under wartime conditions, I remember this place so well before the war." She then ran over the coding system, the

call-up sign, and then she said "Tomorrow I start work."
This meant working in a taverna as a waitress, and of course
in the evening she would do a spot of dancing with the locals
and the German soldiers.

Her first evening was very rewarding, as she waited on the
tables she joked with the Germans and showed them polite
aimiable attention, plus the occasional dance.

It was in the early hours of the morning, that one of the
German soldiers under the influence of drink, had his arm
around her. It was then that she whispered in his ear and
speaking in German she said "I hope your regiment will not
be moving on."

He looked at her and said "Why do you ask?"

Denise flapped her eyes, smiled and put her head against
his and said "Because now that I have got to know you I
don't want you to go." She then continued "Perhaps after
the war we can meet and get married. I would love to live in
Germany."

He was flattered to think that this gorgeous Greek girl
fancied him, so he volunteered a little information. "To tell
you the truth we are all moving to Patras where there will be
troopships to transport us to Návpaktos." His voice then
faded out as his eyes slowly closed.

She then helped him to his feet, as she called Nicol the
owner of the taverna who came to her aid and helped to get
the German soldier out of his taverna, where they left him to
struggle on his own down the street. It was not long before
other Germans equally as drunk came down and joined him.

Once back inside Nicol said to Denise "Well what did you
learn from him?"

In quiet surroundings she explained to him what the
German had said. Such information was then passed onto the
resistance. Denise was also able to make the necessary contact
with London and inform them of this information. When
London checked this out, it made sense, because they had
some knowledge of a build-up of ships, but did not know just
when the big move would start. With this knowledge they
now made preparations to advance further up the Greek
mainland because it was now obvious that the German Army
was making their retreat over to Bríndisi in Italy.

In the following few days, troops and equipment were moving to Patras, and when all was ready for the troops to move a well-planned raid was made by the Allies and vast German losses were suffered, plus the entire transport ships were destroyed. Denise was overjoyed to think that she had contributed to this successful operation. However the German troops and heavy equipment now at Návpaktos started to move towards Mesolóngion, and then making its way to Arta.

At this stage of the operations, Denise needed to move on, so arrangements were made for her to travel to Prévaza by a Greek fishing ship. This was not difficult, but she would then be in the thick of the German Army. Prévaza is a large port where normally large vessels and ferries moved in and out. This was a main route to Igoumenitsa, and she thought if she could get yet another fishing boat to take her to Igoumenitsa, she would be at the main port where the German Army and its heavy vehicles would be in order to cross over to the island of Corfu, and then to Bríndisi in Italy — this all made sense to Denise.

She made contact with London and asked for their agreement. Within two hours she was instructed to do as she had planned.

The following few days passed without interruption, but during her travels she learned of a certain German officer whose atrocities were being noted; his name of course was none other than Heidrick Von Steinrickter, and he was apparently stationed at Arta.

Now came the time for Denise to decide what she should do. Should she make her way to Arta and get the revenge that she had planned all that time ago, or stay in Igoumenitsa as agreed by London, in order that she would pass on information of German movements? She gave the matter a great deal of thought. Her heart was thinking of Tom. Then she remembered what she was told during one of her interviews, and that was not to jeopardise others for her own desires, and it was with this in mind that she decided to stay in Igoumenitsa.

The Greeks now appeared to be relaxed as though they

were aware of the fact that the Germans were losing and were on the retreat. Denise found the atmosphere very pleasant, but on no account could she afford to lack attention to the job she had been sent to do. Although the Germans' moral was low, she still had to appear as though she wanted them to win. She was now employed in an office as a clerk for a large transport company, and only one member of the company was aware of her SOE connections. It was through various pieces of information obtained through working in this company, that she was able to pass this information on to London where it was used to the Allies' advantage — such as bombing more accurately.

Denise, although not under suspicion, did find it difficult to keep the odd German wolf at bay. She did not wish to appear obstructive or objectionable to their advances.

Two months had passed, when suddenly a vast German retreat was on, mainly due to information being divulged to the Allies. Denise at this point was not under suspicion. She also understood that a certain German officer was intending to get his army and heavy vehicles transported from Igoumenitsa to the Corfu port, and Denise found out that the coward he was, he was intending to be on the first crossing. She frantically called up London and said "I feel it necessary that I should now go to Corfu." When asked why she said "I need to be there to interfere with the Germans' operation of their getting to Italy."

Finally London agreed, and so she made preparations to travel on a fishing ship which was owned by a good Greek by the name of Alex. He was very good looking, and his age was around forty-five, but a very happily married man with two children, and his home was of course on Corfu in the village of Benitsa, which was known for its fishing activities and was positioned on the east side of the island, about seven miles from Corfu town.

Alex arranged for Denise to stay with a family that could be trusted in Corfu town. The street was called Marasli, and the family name was Kepayia. After introducing her to the family, Alex made his way back to Benitsa. It was during dinner that it was decided that Denise should be employed in the family's clothes shop, which was situated in the heart of the town; and so it was she was able to earn her keep and could transmit whatever she wished from an empty shop close by that had been bombed, and therefore if ever detected by the Germans the family would not be involved. This was agreed, and with the skills of Denise the likelihood of her being caught was negligible.

She had very little to report at first, and she was enjoying some life on the island, when suddenly she became aware that an armada of ships was coming to Corfu. She frantically called up London and informed them of the situation, and asked what should she do. Their reply was "Sit tight but keep a close eye on everything."

After a further week, she got impatient and spent the odd evening in a cafe at the Volta at the Liston. These are arcades which face the Spianada which were built by the French during their occupation in Napoleon's time. There are identical arcades in the Rue de Rivoli in Paris. She sat always at the same table if possible, and drank always a little Greek wine with a fancy Greek pastry, under the ornate hanging metal lights, which years ago were lit by gas. It was during one of these evenings that several German officers occupied the tables, and when she arrived there was nowhere to sit. It was so obvious to them that one polite officer offered his seat and asked her to join them. He himself went on his way and Denise grabbed the opportunity of being with them.

They could not speak Greek and she made out that she could not speak German which made the situation easy for Denise. They were just trying to relax and it was during their moments of relaxation that they let out vital information. She appeared to them not to know what they were saying just in case they were trying to find out if what they were saying was of interest to her, so she ignored them and only smiled to be polite. She remained at the table for about half an hour, by which time only two officers remained, their conversation was about their home in Germany. In fact they both came from Munich and occasionally they looked at her and smiled. It was at this point that Denise was about to get up, when suddenly after a long gap in their conversation one of them mentioned Heidrick Von Steinrickter, but not in a favourable way. It was clear also that they wanted the war to end and their comments indicated that if only the Allies were aware of certain facts, then Germany would be at a loss in Greece and in Italy, and their dislike of Von Steinrickter was clearly understood. His treachery towards the Allies had caused much harm to his own men. But where was he? That's what mattered to Denise. So she decided to stay a little longer. The officers ordered further drinks and it was during a lull in their conversation that one of them said "And to think that bastard Steinrickter is going to be billeted in a villa in the grounds of the Achillion Palace, which is at the moment being used as a hospital." Then the other officer said "Where is the Achillion Palace?" His friend said "It's the palace that the Empress of Austria built way back in 1890 as her summer retreat, and it's situated in a village called Gastoúri."

At that moment Denise decided to move on in case it looked too suspicious her sitting for such a long while, so she moved away silently without saying a word which gave her the opportunity to talk with Costas who was one of the waiters. She felt the evening had been all worthwhile.

As she made her way home, she wondered just how she could meet this Von Steinrickter, and as she strolled through the streets towards Roco Square which was almost deserted, suddenly she turned into Marasli Street where she was staying.

The next day was Sunday which meant that time was her own, and so in relaxed mood she and her friend called Zoi decided to spend the day together. Zoi was an attractive dark-haired girl with a very slim figure. She was a nurse and she was employed as a staff nurse at the Achillion Palace, now being used as a hospital. They made their way towards the main harbour in Corfu town.

Denise said "Could I come along and see where you work Zoi?"

"Why not my dear" was Zoi's reply.

By this time they had reached the harbour and there were many large vessels.

Whilst they were looking around the harbour, Zoi said "You know Denise I hate the Germans and I would give anything to disrupt their military movements." She paused for a moment then she continued "You know they killed my brother Costas?"

Denise turned her head and looked at Zoi and said "No I did not know that. Why did they do such a thing?"

"Well Costas was running many risks because he was passing valuable information to the resistance and they caught him."

"Then what happened?" said Denise as they continued to walk on.

"Well, you know the old fort?"

"Yes" said Denise.

"Well, Costas used to go there late at night and he would give information to fishing vessels out at sea by signalling with a torch. He was of course caught and questioned. He was tortured, and finally they shot him."

As she was telling Denise this tears flowed down her cheeks.

Denise put her arms around her and said "Well I will carry on where Costas left off."

They then started to walk back into the town. Zoi then said "Why don't we go to Kanoni this afternoon and have a swim?"

"I would like that Zoi, but I have not got a bathing costume."

"That's no problem, you are about my size, so you can have one of mine."

Denise was so excited that she held onto Zoi's arm and the two girls made their way home for a spot of lunch and prepare for the afternoon, laying around on the beach and doing a spot of swimming.

Kanoni is only a walking distance from where they both lived. It was whilst they were having lunch that Denise approached Zoi by saying "Zoi is it possible that in my spare time I could be of use at the hospital in the Achillion Palace?"

Such a request took Zoi by surprise, then looking at Denise she said "If that is what you would like to do then why not?

There are all sorts of jobs that you could assist with, and if it is arranged when I am on duty I for one would love it." Then she continued with a puzzled look on her face "Tell me why do you want to do this?"

Denise then answered "Not only would I be doing some good, I also have other reasons."

The subject was dropped for a little while then Zoi said "Whatever the reason you will be careful, won't you dear?"

"Oh yes, I will be very careful, that I can assure you."

Soon the pair of them were on their way strolling the streets of Corfu and into the well-laid-out Spianada with its large area of grass and trees that were planted by the French during their occupation in the Napoleonic period, also by the British when they too occupied the island. It is here that one can experience riding around in a horse-drawn carriage. Soon the two girls were at the Garitsa seafront boulevard.

The other pleasure whilst at Kanoni is to feast one's eyes on the island of Pondikonissi better known as Mouse Island where stands a church of the Pantokrator built around the 11th century, but Denise was interested in another church just a stone's throw away from Kanoni which covers almost all of a nearer island and that is the Vlacherna Convent. "I would like to visit that church sometime" said Denise.

Now it was time for the two girls to slip off their dresses and into their bathing costumes. They were soon splashing around in the Ionian Sea. It was a hot day and the water was warm. They both enjoyed themselves swimming around and laughing.

There is so much to see on Corfu but in such hostile conditions the pleasure was not to be had — for instance the landing of German tanks on the south of the island will always be remembered by the Corfiots. The Germans drove their heavy trucks along the coast road, and at Parama they demolished an attractive bridge. It was used by the Kaiser Willhelm II when his yacht was moored up at Parama. This destructive attitude towards the Greeks was only to cause bad feeling.

Whilst the girls laid on the beach Zoi said "Tell me have you a boyfriend in England?"

This kind of conversation was bound to arise sometime,

after all Denise was really a very beautiful girl.

Denise sat up right and looked out to sea then she said "Well Zoi, to answer your question. I did have a boyfriend in the RAF, but he was shot down over Germany and was taken prisoner of war and like your brother Costas he also was tortured and killed, and so at this moment in time I have no boyfriend."

Zoi then sat up and she grabbed Denise's arm and said "Is that why you joined the SOE?"

"Yes, that is why and that is why I have to be very careful" she went on to say, "Zoi I need to trust you and I know I can, but whatever I do I will not have you involved."

Zoi then said "But I am involved and you know it, so trust me. I want the Germans out."

Denise then said "You know you asked me why I wanted to help in the Achillion Palace Hospital?"

"Yes" said Zoi.

"Well, I said to you not only would I be doing some good, I also had my reasons and those reasons are that the officer in charge is Heidrick Von Steinrickter and he was the one who tortured and killed my boyfriend. Also the atrocities that he has commited have been unbelievable, and it has been my intention to track him down as well as doing my job, and I understand that he is in the Achillion Palace."

Zoi was horrified but understood and said "I will help you. It will give me great pleasure and satisfaction to have justice done."

She then went on to tell Denise that his quarters are not in the palace but in the villa close to the palace. So Denise agreed to take it easy and take her time to plan meeting him and giving him a terrible death.

After their swim they made their way home feeling very happy. Denise knew now that having Zoi on her side she felt safe, and it was during the following week that Zoi suggested that Denise go with her to the Achillion Palace, which is situated in a small village called Gastoúri. It is a quiet village with a small store and a few villas. There is a taverna for the locals called Spiros's Bar run by a very nice Greek family.

The evening arrived and both girls caught the local bus that runs from Corfu town direct to Gastoúri and turns around at the Achillion Palace main gates. In peacetime the palace was a main tourist attraction and has a museum with valuable items belonging to the late Empress of Austria and the late Kaiser, but now of course all such valuable items have been carefully hidden away.

Both girls made their way through the main gates up the long drive to the entrance. The first thing you notice once inside is the huge hall and the vast stairway which separates, with one stairway going to the left and the other to the right, which brings you onto the first floor. The enormous tapestry on the first landing is of Achilles in his chariot during a battle dragging his enemy along the ground by his legs. The ground floor and the first floor were being used for the injured soldiers.

Zoi took Denise to an office where she introduced her to an official and explained to her that Denise wished to offer her services to do anything that may help in her spare time. The offer was accepted and so various duties were discussed, which Denise accepted. She was shown around the palace which impressed her very much.

She said to Zoi "You know when this war is over I will return — you can depend on it."

Finally, both girls stood on the steps of the main entrance. Zoi then said "You see that villa over there?"

"Yes" said Denise.

"Well it was built by the empress to house the man who would keep an eye on the palace and the staff, and next to it are the stables for the empress' horses and carriages."

Denise was looking at the villa then she said "That's all very interesting."

Then Zoi said "Ah but the interesting thing is that your Heidrick Von Steinrickter is housed in that villa."

"Ah, now that *is* interesting," said Denise, and at that moment a staff car drove up to the villa door, and out stepped Von Steinrickter.

Zoi then said "And that is 'you know who'."

He was rather smartly dressed and slim, but a vain-looking man. Everything about him was neat and tidy, but one could see the vanity of this creature. He looked every inch a Nazi and you could see instantly a really cold callous human being.

Denise said, with a very serious look on her face, "He is no match for me. I will have his guts for garters."

Zoi then said "What do you mean?"

"I will be just plain hard to get and so it will all be on my terms that our love affair will be based. He is not a man to accept being refused. It will first of all hurt his pride. Then when he wins me over, he will revert to a cruel nature of love. This will of course blind his better judgement, so that when he feels that he can do anything when making violent love, it will be then when I shall strike and I promise you Zoi that when he is helpless I will inform him as to whom I am and why I am going to kill him, and believe me Zoi his death will be a painful and bloody death which I shall take endless time before finally finishing him off."

Poor Zoi was horrified to what Denise had just told her and so she said "I am sure what you have just said you will be able to carry out, and I really do wish you all the luck in the world, and if I can be of any use please do not hesitate to ask me."

As the next few days passed, Denise was sending certain information about German movements to Athens, and this information was of great assistance to the Allies. Apparently Berlin was becoming annoyed with Von Steinrickter — also his men were beginning to turn against him.

It was when Denise and Zoi had arranged to dine at Spiros's taverna one evening — it was warm and a cloudless night. The moon shone down on the Ionian Sea. Far in the distance the Greek mainland could be seen. The whole atmosphere was very romantic. Both Zoi and Denise chose their table wisely and had of course ordered their meal. Zoi decided to have meat, and Denise ordered fish. Their choice of wine was a bottle of Porto Carras, which is a white wine. The two girls were chatting away, when suddenly Heidrick Von Steinrickter appeared with other officers. The table they decided to have was in full view of the girls. He made a point of constantly looking at Denise, and it was not long before he made his way over to their table. He first of all stood in silence.

Then Denise said "You want something?"

He could not understand Greek very well but he could tell that whatever she said was somewhat objectionable. He tried again this time with a smile and indicated that they both join him at his table as his guests, but once again it was obvious that he had been rejected. This hurt his pride and he stormed back to his table.

During the evening, he and his fellow officers became objectionable to other diners. They started to sing Nazi songs and thumped the table. By this time both Denise and Zoi decided to go.

The following evening Denise returned to the Achillion Palace to help with the patients in the hospital. Again Von Steinrickter neglected his duties in order to visit the hospital as he had become aware that certain evenings she attended the patients. He made a nuisance of himself as he persistently interrupted her duties in order to hold a conversation with her and to make a date again. It was obvious to him that she wanted nothing to do with him. He found her as a most outstanding beautiful, natural, blonde with a figure he could not resist. Her poise was that of an aristocrat. As she glided along, he found it impossible to take his eyes off her, and whilst he was there one of his staff was talking to him on something of a military importance. In fact he told the officer to attend to the matter himself. Denise by this time had disappeared. He tried hard to find her but failed miserably. But Denise could see him, and with a grin on her face she thought 'I'll get you, you swine'.

# CHAPTER 6

During the following days, Heidrick spent a lot of time trying to see if he could catch Denise. In fact he should have been at a meeting on one occasion discussing the movements of German troops that were being shipped from the mainland of Greece to Corfu — this movement was of vital importance, and his absence was noted.

That same week, he and fellow officers were in Corfu town drinking in a cafe, when one of the officers spotted Denise walking across the grass towards the road leading to St. Spyridon Church. His remark was "Look at that beauty. What would I like to do with her!"

Heidrick looked in the direction the officer was pointing and said "Excuse me. I'll be back."

In his haste he pushed into several Greeks.

Denise was aware of him, so she made sure he could still see her in the distance.

Then he bumped into a Greek pushing a barrow. By the time he looked around she had disappeared. He returned to the cafe very much out of breath. He was becoming obsessed with her, and it clouded his mind that should have been on more important and vital things.

Finally, Denise decided to close in on him; but before doing so she was called to a resistance meeting which was to discuss the blocking of any further German troops landing on Corfu. Which meant that all German troops left on the mainland would be captured and made prisoners of war. Regarding the remaining troops on Corfu, their escape to Brindisi, the port in Italy, would be stopped. This meant a battle would be fought on Corfu and the resistance would overpower the German troops. It would of course be a bloody battle, but the Greeks knew that it was only a matter of time before the Allies would land on the island. An order came from Berlin that because of Heidrick's neglect and incompetence of causing the failure of the Germans' control in Greece, that they wanted him arrested. This information was picked up by the resistance, and Denise thought how could she get her revenge before he was taken back to German?

As for Heidrick, he was now in a panic situation. What could he do? He realised that he would be put on trial, and of course finally shot.

Denise now thought should she finish him off or leave it to the resistance, because no reprisals would be made should he be killed?

However whilst he was seeking a way out, Denise made her move. She informed the resistance of her plan and it was that she would dine with him on a night when the Allies were about to move from the mainland of Greece over to Corfu. The Germans' escape route to Brindisi would be blocked by the Greek resistance, and Denise would finally tempt Heidrick to accompany her to her flat in Corfu town. This plan was approved by the resistance, of which they also would be at hand.

The next day she was in luck, for whilst she was shopping in town, Heidrick also was in town — he was trying to contact a friend who could help him to escape to Ancona, which is on the east side of Italy. Denise made it possible for him to see her and naturally he made his way over to her.

They came face to face and he said "Please may I talk with you?"

Denise then said, "Yes if you wish."

He then appeared to be stuck for words. He then smiled and said "Would you join me in this cafe for coffee?"

She looked him straight in the eye and said "Well I have something that I must do. I'm sorry but I cannot."

He then said "Would you please have dinner with me tonight in the restaurant at the Liston?"

She took her time and said "Alright, but what time?"

He answered quickly, "Shall we say around seven!"

"Very well" said Denise.

They parted. He was of course very pleased with himself, and she knew what she had in mind for him after dinner.

She then promptly contacted the resistance and informed them of her movements that evening, and they agreed to go along with her plan.

The day seemed to drag on, and Denise contacted her friend Zoi to let her know of the dangerous plan she had in mind that evening.

Zoi said "Denise do be careful. He is a man not to be trusted."

"I understand" said Denise.

Soon the evening arrived. It was very warm and she had decided to wear something rather sexy and flimsy so that it flowed with every movement she made — in fact you could almost see through it in certain lights.

Heidrick arrived promptly on time, and a few minutes later Denise arrived looking extremely attractive. He was of course very attentive and very polite. The conversation was one of flattery. He was not aware of Denise's connections with the resistance, or of her being in the SOE. He of course, was playing with death. He was, in no time at all, making advances to her, and she was, of course, leading him on. He also had no idea that she was aware that Berlin had ordered for him to be arrested.

During the day, he had met his friend and arrangements had been made for his escape the next day. So he was feeling on top of the world and to think that he was now dining the girl of his dreams — what more could her wish for? — other than sex with her to the limit.

As the evening rolled on, he became more familiar towards her. He said "You know you are a very beautiful young lady."

She said "I understand what you are saying, but my German is not good."

He laughed and said "After the meal will you come back to my villa in Gastoúri?"

She smiled and said "No, but perhaps you would come to my apartment here in town?"

Of which he thought would be better than going back to his villa, and so he said "Yes of course, and perhaps we can have coffee and a little love, yes?"

She then said, "Yes I would like that."

Before they left the restaurant, she looked around for one of the resistance men. But no one was around. She was a little worried and thought if she had no help then it was up to her to finish him off. She knew she had the guts, but did not really want to soil her hands over such a villain. However the walk from the restaurant to her apartment was not a long one, and so they arrived very quickly, and to her relief when she entered the street she caught sight of a member of the resistance. She began to relax as they walked closer to her apartment. They proceeded up the stairs. She placed the key in the door and soon they both entered. Once inside she offered Heidrick a drink — which he accepted. He made himself comfortable on the settee, and she joined him. Within moments his hands began to wander. She closed her eyes and felt a shiver run down her spine. He then pulled her towards him to kiss her passionately. At that moment she offered him another drink — which he accepted.

After several drinks he thought he was on a good thing and fancied his chances. The evening was working towards intimacy with sex. He tried to pull her down onto the settee. She pulled away, but he grabbed her and used violence. She slapped his face. He staggered across the room and grabbed her again. His hands dug into her arms. It was painful.

He then said, "You are very beautiful, but you are still a common tart just playing hard to get."

She was then close to him and so she had the opportunity of bringing her knee up into his crotch. He screamed out and doubled up in pain. She then grabbed him by the throat. She very nearly choked him. He struggled for his breath. Then she told him about Tom. He vaguely remembered Tom. By then she twisted his arm up his back to the point of breaking it. She really gave him a terrible time. She relaxed for a second and he grabbed her arm to pull her down. She turned sharply and grabbed a knife. With a swift movement she cut his hand with such force that all his fingers were severed from his hand. He screamed out in horror. Blood flowed like water. Then she brought the knife across his face which disfigured him instantly. Her temper was high, and she was about to plunge the knife into his heart, when the door was pushed open and in came three resistance men.

Two of them grabbed Heidrick and the other asked Denise "Are you alright?"

She was now breathing deeply and said "Yes, I am alright thank you."

As for Heidrick, he thought that they had come to rescue him, but he soon found out that they were resistance men and his hopes faded as they took him out of Denise's apartment and dragged him to an awaiting car. They then drove off to Kanoni where they beat him up. He was by this time bleeding very badly. They then dragged him to a high point and then threw him over onto the rocks and sea below. His body was smashed to pieces. Their job was now done, and so they moved off and finally returned to Denise's apartment.

On their arrival they found her composed and grateful that it had not been up to her to finally kill him.

Spiros was the first to speak. "The necessary deed has been done. We threw his battered body over the rocks and into the sea at Kanoni. His body will be found, but we are all in the clear."

Another Greek, by the name of Nicol, said "There will not be any reprisals, as his fellow officers will be pleased to know that he is dead, and the German high command will be pleased back in Berlin."

Spiros then said "We are pleased that you did not jeopardise the resistance operation just to satisfy your own wishes. We will remember you for this."

The resistance men then left.

When the next day arrived, the sun was warm, the sky was blue and not a cloud to be seen. As she gazed out of her window, her thoughts were mainly on the future and what it had in store for her. So quickly into the bathroom for a shower, then to the make-up box; a quick cup of tea and another look out of her window to the main road that took traffic out of the town and passed the old fort and on to the south of the island. She then looked below onto a garden that needed attention; such as the grass wanted cutting and the flowerbeds needed a great deal to be done to them; and looking further across the main road one could see the Ionian Sea, and in the distance was the Greek mainland, and further to the north one could see the coast of Albania.

Within a few weeks, the Allies had landed on Corfu and the remaining Germans were taken prisoner. Also the Allies had landed in Italy. So much rejoicing took place on Corfu.

It was an island that Denise had fallen in love with and hoped that one day she would return and enjoy it all in peacetime conditions; but what she had made whilst she was there was many friends, and Zoi was top of her list.

With her work for the SOE now finished, arrangements were being made for her to return to Blighty; and as the days went by she just could not wait to be on her way. And so the final day came for her to be put on a plane back to Cyprus, and from there she was flown to England where she was met by a member of the SOE and taken straight to their headquarters.

She was met by the officer who last saw her before she left for Greece. He came forward and put his arms around her and said "Denise you were wonderful, you came up to all our expectations and I for one am very proud to have worked with you." He released his hold on her then continued, "You have been mentioned regarding the award of the OBE." He then said "I am so glad that you did not jeopardize any operation for your own desires of revenge."

She looked at him with a very serious expression and said "I remembered what you said Sir, and that was when the time comes for serious descisions, the obvious was plain commonsense and it paid off."

"Well my dear, the old saying is ever true, 'right will prevail'."

They then walked among other members of the department.

# CHAPTER 7

It was now 1945, and hostilities had ceased regarding the war with Germany and Italy, and so it was obvious that the SOE would be disbanded.

Denise was to return home to Blackpool. The whole journey brought back old memories of Tom and Ruth, and as the train sped on its way, destruction could be seen which was the price one pays for peace. Not only England, but all Europe was picking up the pieces, and people were hoping to reshape their lives and hoped it would never happen again.

In no time at all, Denise was stepping off the train. She then made her way to the bus stop. It all looked so different. Everybody seemed in a hurry as though they could not wait to get on with their lives.

The bus arrived and with further memories running through her mind, she was soon at her destination. She slowly walked towards where she lived. When her house came into view, it was like a breath of fresh air. The road was quiet and very peaceful with its tall trees either side of the road; and as she turned into the entrance of the old home, she experienced a lump in her throat. Then hurriedly she rushed to the door. It opened with her mother standing there with outstretched arms and tears flowing down her cheeks.

As she flung her arms around her daughter she said "Welcome home darling."

Tears also were clearly seen pouring down Denise's face.

As they entered the hallway, her father embraced her and said "I have missed you darling." His eyes were full and slightly red.

Then her sister Mary cuddled her, and as they all wiped their tears from their eyes, her mother said "I'll put the kettle on."

Her father looked at her and said "Your mother has not changed, the tea pot is always number one priority."

They then all laughed as she put her small humble suitcase down in the hall. The phone rang. She picked it up and after a few exchanges of words she said "Dad, it's for you."

Whilst he was on the phone, the two sisters went into the kitchen where mother was preparing the tea.

Then their father came in and said "You will have to excuse me for a while, I have to make a call, but it won't take long."

Denise then said "Nothing has changed."

As her father made his way out, after giving mother a kiss, all three females sat down in the large kitchen and Mary said "We have all been so very worried about you dear. We realised the dangerous job that you were engaged on. What I want to know now is what have you in mind to do for the future? Are you returning to show business?"

Her mother then said "Yes darling, what are you going to do?"

"Well" said Denise, "I have been giving the matter some thought, and I think I will from now on stick around and perhaps find a job in a clothes shop."

"Well, there is always Dawson's in High Street" said Mary.

"That is not a bad idea. I will try them next week" said Denise.

Much happiness was had in the family over the following days. Then after the weekend, Denise made her way to Dawson's in High Street. It was just a shot in the dark. She walked straight through the main entrance which she had done many times before the war. She then made for the stairway to the first floor. Then she passed the furniture department and on to the acounts department, and finally she stopped at the reception desk where a young lady said "Can I help you?"

"I hope so. I am looking for employment. Can you tell me who I should see?"

The young lady looked Denise up and down then said, "Will you sit down there and wait for a moment." The young girl disappeared — it seemed ages before she returned.

Then a much older lady arrived and said "Hello, will you come this way."

They walked into an office which was very smart and clean with a great many filing cabinets.

She was then asked to sit down opposite the lady who said, "What is your name dear?"

"My name is Denise Povey. I am single and I live locally, and my age is twenty-three."

The lady looked a kind person, but obviously the store came first and so she said to Denise "That's nice to know, but can you tell me more about yourself?"

The lady looked at Denise with interest and so Denise felt at ease, so she said "Well, during my school years I took an interest in dancing, and so I left school and joined a dancing school, and finally I went into show business. I was a chorus girl engaged in shows in London and Southern England. During the war I joined ENSA and this took me to India. When I returned to England, I applied and was accepted, after military training, to join the SOE. I was sent to Greece and I worked with the Greek resistance, and now with the war over I am looking for employment on a more permanent basis."

The lady was so surprised with what Denise was saying, that her eyes were of a fixed stare and her mouth was permanently open. The pen she had in her hand for making notes was poised at a fixed angle. She then pulled herself together and said "Well my dear you have been very busy and obviously very conscientious towards things, which makes you a company person. What can I say to a young lady who has achieved so much?" She paused for a moment and then said "Normally one fills in an application form giving details of one's CV, but I think we can skip such formalities at this stage. I will of course ask you to fill in such a form giving your name and address and age, together with all that you have told me so far, and I think we need not have any further interviews." She finished writing her notes and then she said "Tell me what department had you in mind to work in?"

To Denise's surprise it looked as though she had got herself a job, so she answered "I think I would prefer to work in your fashion department."

"Well my dear, with your beauty and presentation I think that would be an excellent thought." The lady then gave Denise a form and said "Just fill this in and let us have it back. We will be offering you employment with this store. You will be hearing from us."

All that remained was for a few pleasant words to be exchanged, then to depart.

Denise walked out of the store feeling very happy, and when she arrived home she broke the good news to her parents that she had found a job; and so that evening they celebrated by going to a local restaurant and enjoying themselves.

As the following weeks passed with Denise now employed in Dawson's store, the family was able to settle down to a normal way of life. It was during a normal day's work at Dawson's that things were about to change for Denise.

Half-way through this particular morning a young man was seen wandering around the store. He was handsome and in his early twenties. His hair was dark and wavy, and he had very sharp features. He was also alone. It was obvious that he was making his way to the gentleman's department — well that would be the normal impression, but instead he wandered around the ladies' fashions. His height was a little under six feet, and as he strolled around, his eyes became fixed on Denise. He soon walked towards her and started chatting her up. Romance was on his mind, but Denise had no intention of allowing love or sex to come between her and her future.

He started to make conversation by saying "You are very attractive. You should be in show business."

Denise took this compliment in her stride and said "Really, why are you in show business?"

He answered quickly, "No, it's just that you are so beautiful."

"Thank you" she said.

Then he asked her "Would you have dinner with me tonight?"

She said "Where have you in mind?"

"There is a very nice restaurant on the seafront called Power's."

"Alright, that would be nice thank you" she said.

He then suggested that he meet her outside the store, and the arrangement was made for 6 o'clock.

She smiled and he said "That's fine. See you at six then."

When she finished work, she strolled outside and waited. He soon made an appearance. He seemed rather shy, but very pleasant. He was smartly dressed and so they made their way to the seafront.

They soon arrived at the restaurant. Once inside, and sitting at a table, he made several overtures to her which she accepted pleasantly, but Denise had no intention of allowing a love affair to begin.

The evening meal was a great success, and on the table Denise noticed a card concerning a beauty contest. It was being sponsored by several restaurants, one of which was Power's Restaurant; and so before leaving the young man suggested "Why don't you put your name down? I think you would win."

She laughed and said "I think not."

"Oh, don't be so modest. You are sure to win."

It made Denise think, and as they got up to go out he said "Let's get an application form for entering you. What have you got to lose?"

His encouragement made her think and she said "All right. Why not!"

So before leaving, he obtained the necessary form. It was simple enough to fill in, and so as they strolled along the promenade they found a seat and he said "I have a pen, so why not fill the form in now and post it?"

Which is what she did.

The evening ended very pleasantly and he asked her "Can I see you again?"

She said "If you wish, but please do not misunderstand me, but I have no intentions of romance. Do you understand?"

He looked rather sad but said, "I understand there has been someone else, I think?"

She said "Yes, and I have not got over it."

He then said "Can we be friends?"

"Of course" was her reply, but it was obvious to him that to continue the friendship it would only end up in tears as far as he was concerned, and so the relationship was short-lived.

As the days went by, she did often think about him. They had exchanged names and addresses, but that was all. It was very sad, but some good came out of meeting him, because within a couple of weeks since they met, she did receive a letter from the beauty contest officials who asked her to send them a photograph of herself. She discussed it all with her parents, and they agreed that it would do no harm to send the photograph and see what became of it all. So she had a studio photograph taken of herself in a bathing costume as they had requested.

During the following week she received instructions regarding an interview, and so one afternoon she requested to have time off — and it was granted. She arrived at the local county hall where all the contestants congregated. It was of course very noisy with all the chatter, but it was amusing.

Then, one by one, they were asked to go to a desk which was at one end of the hall, where there sat three gentlemen and a lady with notepaper and pen in front of them. They asked for silence and then proceeded to interview each competitor. The whole procedure was one of a very serious nature, after all, such an event had not taken place since 1938. They were also told about the procedure and that it would take place at the end of the month. It would be held in the open grounds of the gardens close to the seafront. Should the weather not be favourable, it would then be held in the dance hall close by. They were then told of what they were to do, and four judges would pick the 1st, 2nd and 3rd. The prize for the 1st was £1,000; the 2nd was £500; and the 3rd was to be £200. All would of course also receive some fashionable clothes.

And so it was all set. There were twenty contestants between the ages of eighteen and thirty. Denise thought that at least accepting that evening out with that young man she was given the chance to go into the competition.

The day for the competition — the weather was great. There was sun and blue skies, and a lot of holiday-makers ready to join into the spirit of things. Denise's mother and sister were there, but her father had surgery to attend to, so he was not able to enjoy the event; and somewhere in the crowd was the young man who had encouraged Denise to have a go.

She was beautifully made up by a local beauty parlour — as all contestants were. The clothes they wore, to their surprise, were donated by several ladies' fashion shops, and their hair arranged by two local hairdressing parlours. The crowds were now seated, and the walkway platform, lined with a red carpet, awaited the beauties to come on and do their very best. The first to take her walk was dressed in a very loose and colourful short dress. Her hair was dark and hanging on her shoulders. Her walk was very nice, but of course it being her first appearance in public she was a novice; but for all that she did look competitive and the appreciation from the audience was of great encouragement and everybody settled down to enjoy this competition, wondering who would win. There were five young ladies to go. Then on walked Denise dressed in a navy two-piece tailored suit with a white blouse folded out over the collar of the jacket, which had elbow-length sleeves. She wore no stockings, but her legs were well tanned a lovely shade of brown. She wore no hat, and her outstanding natural blonde hair, pulled up from her neck, gave her an elegant look coupled with the way she held herself up high as she walked in a very sexy manner in her high black court leather shoes. Her face had a serious expression not normally shown on a mannequin. They usually have a slight smile, but Denise was something different — her elegant and slimline waist, coupled with a very sexy swing, found only in professional dancers.

She paused at the end of the walkway, and turned slowly, but with confidence. As she walked back and out of sight, her presence commanded silence and only sighs could be heard as she passed the audience, after which voices were raised and hands were clapped. She had obviously come over big with the public. Her stage experience had paid off. There was of course a slight lull.

Then the competition was to be completed by the girls wearing bathing costumes. Each and every one of them had attractive features and very good body lines, but when Denise appeared it was obvious to the audience as to who was the winner. Her costume left nothing to the imagination — its colour was of Cambridge blue. She had blue high-heeled shoes, and her hair was this time shoulder-length with a high wave over her forehead. She was of course a complete knockout. The decision of the judges was overwhelming. They all voted Denise the winner. The crowds stood up and cheered as Denise walked up to the mayor. First he put the wide blue silk sash around her shoulders which read 'Blackpool Beauty Queen' and then she was handed a cheque for £1,000. He then kissed her and congratulated her on her victory.

Many people came up to her to congratulate her and passed many flattering words. There were so many around her that she was overwhelmed. Then as she glanced around she caught sight of the young man that she owed it all to. She tried to make her way to him, but he disappeared in the crowd. Her mother by this time was holding her arm and her sister was showing such feeling of proudness after the crowds had dispersed and all was over. An evening dinner had been arranged for all of those who had taken part in the competition. It surely was a day to be remembered.

The next day was Sunday, and it gave Denise time to collect her thoughts. It was obvious that having won the title of a beauty queen, she would be expected to attend all sorts of things such as hospitals, old folks' homes and the usual publicity activities, and who knows with her dancing career in the past, show business agents would be on the lookout?

But Denise sat down that Sunday and said to her parents and sister "You are all probably wondering what I may want to do in the future now that I have been this successful?"

Her mother then said "Yes dear, it had crossed our minds."

"Well, let me tell you this, I have no intentions of going back to the stage and getting involved making money for others, to say nothing of all the travelling around that is demanded — no matter what money is offered."

Her father then said "That's all very well my dear, but at one time your heart was set on a dancing and show business career. What's happened to make you change your mind?"

Denise first of all looked at her father and her mother, also her sister. She then held her mother's hand and said "The war has changed me completely, for I have seen much suffering and so much violence to last me a lifetime. I have also walked with death and I was trained to kill like a man. I have had love in my heart and revenge has run deep in my soul. I have seen poverty, greed and ambition to such standards that I never thought human beings had it in them to commit such atrocities." She paused for a moment then she continued "It is therefore my intention to become very rich, and the best way I can do this is to own my own fashion shop. I will use my charm and the beauty that you Mum and Dad gave me to manipulate business affairs that I will come in contact with, because I am going to be so ambitious, and I will use all my wits. But I will take my time and think carefully every move I make here, and if possible, abroad. America for instance has not suffered as we and other countries have, so they will be more relaxed; but I shall take advantage of other countries such as Italy, Greece and even Germany, who have a money problem. I will tempt them with exceptionally good deals when buying their products to sell."

Her father interrupted her by saying "You my dear, have given this matter a great deal of thought, this I can clearly see, and if you handle it just as you say with care, I can see only one way for you to go, and that is up, and I think you have the guts to do it."

"Thank you Dad, I appreciate what you have just said."

Her sister put her arms around her and said "Oh Denise, I just know you are going to make it."

Her mother cuddled her and said "I'll go and make a pot of tea."

Whilst her mother was in the kitchen, her father said "What will you use for money dear?"

"Well Dad, there is the thousand pounds I have just won. I will carry on at the store for a time getting to know the business and the buyers, and when the time is right I will approach the bank for a bank loan. I will then rent some premises and set up my first shop."

"Well darling, if you need a little more money, you know your mother and I will help you."

"Thanks Dad, but I do want to do it all on my own."

At this point in came mother with the tea.

The following day started with an overcast in the weather. It was rather cloudy and the temperature was down a little.

Denise arrived at the store and was requested to see the store manager. She thought 'Oh dear. What now?' She walked into his office and there he sat with a very serious look on his face.

"Sit down Denise. Tell me with the success of being a beauty queen, what are your intentions in the immediate future?"

Denise answered swiftly. "Well since you ask me I do assume that you are thinking that I will be seeking other employment?"

"Well yes" he said.

"Well I can assure you that I have no plans in finding another job. Does that answer your question?"

"Well, not really, for I am sure you will be expected to get involved in publicity matters, and no doubt you will be asking for time off from time to time. It may be to the store's advantage to have a winner of the beauty contest, but the store will be expected to contribute in some way I'm sure."

The tone of his voice was not a pleasing one so she said "I have no intention of getting involved with anything. As far as I am concerned, I won a competition and that is all. There were no pre-arranged deals that I would be committed to, should I win. I was fully aware as it was pointed out at the time of taking part in such a contest, but as it was put to me it only meant that should I win it could be to my advantage. Now that could mean anything. So I can assure you that I am at present employed in your ladies' fashion department, so if that is all then I will return to my department?"

He looked more relaxed and stood up from his desk and put out his hand and said "Thank you Denise. I will now be able to put the directors' minds at ease, and thank you for coming and explaining your intentions."

She then got up and walked out of his office and back to her department.

As the week progressed, she was contacted by various people who were involved with the competition, but her answer was always the same — "I have no wish for further involvement concerning the contest." Finally she was left alone.

Winter was now not far away, and she was really pleased that she had a local job, with regular pay. Her mind of course was still on owning her own shop, and when 1950 arrived, January was not too bad a month regarding the weather — unlike 1947 when it was the worst winter for many years. Roads from north to south were blocked, and coal was being rationed at the gasworks, just when the people were making a recovery from the war.

## CHAPTER 8

Denise was now thinking that 1950 would be a good year to start up on her own. The £1,000 she won in the beauty contest had been invested, and so it had made a little interest, and of course the banks at that time were prepared to loan cash if you had collateral. She also noticed that a certain shop that had been damaged during the war had now been repaired and painted. It was ideal for a ladies' clothes shop — it was in an ideal position in High Street, and it was available for renting on an annual basis.

She talked it over with her parents, who agreed with her idea on principle. And her sister suggested that she could help in the shop. All it needed was for her to approach the bank manager, which is what she did, and a date was made for her to see him.

She arrived at the bank for a 10 o'clock appointment. He was of course a very pleasant person in his mid-fifties, and he politely asked her to sit down.

He then started by saying "What can we do for you Miss Povey?"

Denise felt relaxed in his company and said "Well I am at present working at Dawson's store in their ladies' clothes department, and it has been my intention since the war to own my own clothes shop, and eventually to own several if possible."

The manager took a good look at her and said "That's being very ambitious, but I can see that you are a very determined young lady, which is in your favour to start with. Your ideas are no doubt good, and having met you I can see you are fashion-minded. He then took a breather and fumbled with a few papers and with pen in hand he said "Now let's get down to facts and figures. What kind of a loan were you wanting, and what collateral can you offer to justify the bank's investment?"

She sat back in the chair, crossed her legs and with a smile on her face she said "As you no doubt are aware, I have a small account with your bank, but I have almost £2,000 in a building society which I wish to use sensibly, purely for the business. I have no collateral, but my father would be willing to offer collateral on my behalf."

"What is your father's business?" he asked.

"He is a doctor."

"Ah," said the manager. "You are of course the daughter of Doctor Povey!"

"That's right" she said.

"Well, that does help in as much that he holds a good position in the community." He paused again and then said "Very well, you have some support — that's fine. Now what I am able to do is advance you on a loan basis. Whatever money you are prepared to put into your business?"

Denise was very pleased and said "That is very kind of you. I will be putting £2,000 to get me off the ground. This will assist in buying clothes racks, shelving, a till and other equipment to set up the shop, and with the loan that your bank will allow me will pay for some stock and go towards the renting of the premises. I will of course furnish the bank with monthly reports on the progress made in the shop."

The bank manager looked rather pleased with what she had told him and then he said "That sounds very satisfactory, and I am sure you will make a go of it."

It now only remained for Denise to proceed with the organising of renting the shop, and for the shopfitters to do the necessary work.

As she left the bank, she walked proudly down High Street, knowing that with what she had in mind needs only to be put into practice.

Within a month she had the shop made ready for customers. She had of course also handed her notice in and so she was now ready to go ahead. Her sister helped her over the weekends putting the final touches for the opening on Monday. That weekend at home they celebrated the future of Denise's new adventure. The shop looked really attractive.

Monday morning arrived and Denise walked from her home to her shop and opened it dead on nine. The shop was full of dresses, blouses, skirts, costumes and jackets — you name it she had got it all in popular sizes and colours. Some of the stock she had bought, and some had been supplied by the manufacturer on a period basis. She had soft background music on the Glen Miller style. The odd thing was, as she opened the door for the public, within seconds a couple of ladies walked in and broused around; and then in came another lady; then a man and his wife. She just could not believe her eyes. She tried to be casual about the whole thing, but within no time at all sales were being made.

The first customer said "It makes a change to see a new shop open with such fine styles and agreeable prices. I hope you will do well my dear."

"Thank you" said Denise.

The next sale the person said "I will have this, but is it possible to get it in green?"

"It can be arranged" said Denise.

"When would you have it in?"

Denise then said "By this coming Saturday."

The lady was surprised and said "Do you need a deposit?"

"Oh no" said Denise.

"Then let me give you my name and address" the lady said.

By the end of the week Denise was re-ordering certain stock that had been sold, and was also ordering new garments that people had remarked about.

The first month of opening had even taken Denise by surprise. It had surpassed all her expectations, her sister had now decided to pack her job in and help in the shop. It was obvious to Denise that the shop was going to be too small but it was early days to do anything about it. She needed more room to accommodate the various seasons, so she thought what she could do was to have another shop close by that did the autumn and winter fashions, and keep the other for spring and summer. So she took it upon herself to make arrangements to see the bank manager again. So a date was made, and she made her way to the bank and through the bank manager's office door again.

And so it was agreed over a cup of coffee that a further loan was permitted. It was obvious that the bank manager was confident of Denise's business ability, and he did agree to help her later on when she needed more money. He was very helpful, which gave her confidence and he put her mind at ease.

As time went by Denise wondered just whatever happened to her friend Ruth Worthy, and it was during an evening meal at home that she said to Mary "I wonder what has happened to Ruth now that the war is over?"

Mary turned her head towards Denise and said "If you have her home address or telephone number why don't you contact her?"

Denise's mother joined in and said "Yes, why not? You were such great friends years ago. Just give her a phone call dear."

So after dinner, Denise decided to do just that, and said "I'll look up her number. I have got it somewhere."

Whilst going through various papers of the past, she came across a photograph of Tom Blake. She sat on the side of her bed caressing the picture. Her thoughts went back to happy days, and as she looked towards the ceiling she said "Oh Tom think of what might have been — you and I happily married, and who knows we may have had lovely children." Then tears came pouring from her beautiful blue eyes.

Then in came Mary and she said "Come on dear, don't upset yourself. What has been done is now in the past. You have all the future to look forward to." She put her arms around Denise and said "You know there could be a very good and handsome fellow somewhere out there. So cheer up and phone Ruth."

But what did the future hold for her, who had show business in her heart, and now a successful business woman?

She got up from the bed and went downstairs to phone — which was in the hall. She dialled and waited. It rang and rang. By this time Mary was standing beside her.

Denise was about to put the phone down when Mary said "Give it a chance."

Then a voice was heard. It was a woman's voice but not Ruth's.

Denise then said "Is that Mrs Worthy?"

The lady then said "Who is that?"

And Denise answered "Oh you don't know me. I am Denise. Ruth and I were together in show business during the war."

There was silence. Then Mrs Worthy said "Oh yes Ruth has spoken about you my dear."

Then Denise said "I would like to talk with Ruth if that is possible?"

"Well my dear, Ruth does not live here any more. She is still in show business as a dancer, and she is on tour with a group. She is also married. Her name is now Gould, and her husband's name is Glen. They have been married five years."

Denise then said "Is there any way that I can contact her?"

"Of course. I will give you her phone number. They live in Preston."

Now that she had Ruth's home number, she returned to the lounge.

"Well dear, did you get what you wanted?" asked her mother.

"Yes Mum, I think I will phone right away."

She then dialled the number given to her and a very pleasant man's voice said "Hello can I help you?"

"Can I speak to Ruth?"

He then said "Well, I'm afraid she is not here — she is on tour. Who is that calling?"

"It's Denise here."

He immediately said "Ah, I know all about you. I am Glen. I don't know when she will be home." There was a pause then he said, "Well to tell you the truth we are separated."

Then Denise interrupted him by saying, "I'm sorry to hear that. I have just spoken to her mother and she did not mention anything about your being separated."

He said "She is aware of the situation, but is rather hoping it will all blow over, but that is not possible. She has no idea that we are planning a divorce — that is, I am anyway. By the way, I have some photographs of you taken during the war. If you would like to have them I will post them on to you, or perhaps we could meet somewhere and I would gladly give them back to you?''

Denise then said ''That's nice. I think it would be better that we meet sometime.''

''Alright, I will be in touch. What is your phone number?''

Denise then returned to the lounge again.

Her mother said ''What is it dear? You look concerned.''

''Well Mum, it seems that Ruth got married, but she is separated from her husband. I have just spoken to him. He also has some old photographs of me and asked me if I would like to have them. I told him I would and he suggested that we meet somewhere. He is going to phone me back sometime.''

''Well my dear, why not meet him and get the pictures back!''

A day or two passed and then she received a call from Glen saying ''Denise, is it possible that we meet in the Lovers' Nest? It's that restaurant in High Street. I don't know if you have been there, but how about around seven tomorrow night and have dinner with me?''

''Yes of course that will be fine. I look forward to it.''

After his call, Denise found herself looking forward to having an evening out with a perfect stranger. She was also looking forward to seeing what pictures he had of her, as she could not remember which ones Ruth had of her, because the last time that they met was when Denise had just joined the SOE, and in her haste she left these photographs with Ruth, when they shared digs together.

The evening arrived and Denise looked beautiful, dressed in a very colourful silky dress with off-the-shoulder design. Her hair being very blonde and hanging on her shoulders. She also wore a pearl necklace and earrings to match. She had a gold bracelet on one wrist, a watch on the other with a very attractive diamond ring on her right hand. In all she looked glamorous.

She walked into the restaurant right on time, only to find that Glen was there waiting. He made his way towards her and was of course spellbound. His eyes were wide open including his mouth as he approached her. He was fascinated by her walk and her figure. Where in the world had he seen such a goddess?

She held out her hand and with her baby-blue eyes and gracious smile she said "Hello Glen, nice to meet you."

He held her hand and gently kissed it. He uttered not a word, then suddenly he said "Hello Denise, nice to meet you also."

They were shown to a very nice secluded table. The waiter was soon at their table asking them if they wished to have a drink before ordering.

Glen looked at Denise and said "Can I tempt you?"

Denise then said "I would like a cream sherry please."

Glen ordered two sherries. It was obvious that the evening was off to a good start.

Denise started the conversation by saying "What a charming restaurant. I have passed it, but I never realised how nice it was inside."

By this time Glen had taken the pictures of Denise out of his pocket.

Denise then said "Before you show me the photos, tell me what went wrong with you and Ruth."

At that moment the waiter came up with the drinks and asked "Can I take your order now Sir?"

Glen looked at him and said "Would you mind waiting for a moment?"

"Not at all Sir. Please take your time and call me when you are ready."

"Yes of course" said Glen. Then Glen said "Now where were we?"

"I asked you what went wrong with you and Ruth?"

Glen let off a sigh and then said "Oh yes, well apparently she was having an affair and it had been going on before we were married and during our engagement period. I was not aware of this."

Denise interrupted him by saying "You were not aware of this?"

"No" said Glen.

"But when did you find out?"

"Well I first noticed that there was something between them at a Christmas party which involved show business people. It was held in an hotel, and whilst the party was in full swing I became aware that Ruth was missing. I wandered around a bit and as I walked along a corridor I became aware of some voices and movement in a bedroom. I paused for a moment and listened. I heard what sounded like two lovers having sexual relationship. My first reaction was to walk on, but then I heard what sounded to be Ruth's voice. I leant towards the door and it was clear to me my thoughts were right, so I opened the door and there on the bed she lay with him on top of her. I stood for a few moments, and then she glanced over his shoulder and looked straight at me. I then closed the door and stood outside for a moment. I knew that if I went back inside I would have killed him."

He stopped talking for a moment then Denise said "How awful Glen. What did you do next?"

"I slowly walked downstairs where all the others were still chatting and drinking. Then as I stood looking out of the window I became aware that they had come down and stood not far from me."

"And then what happened?" asked Denise.

"I turned and faced both of them and said 'You're lucky I did not kill you.' He then said to me 'This is not just an affair today. We have felt this way towards each other for a very long time.' The date he gave was about the time we got engaged. I then stared at both of them and said to him 'You are welcome to her, for if she is prepared to break the marriage vows she will break anything. I could never trust her again'." Glen then held Denise's hand and said "Shall we order?"

Denise said "Why not!"

They looked at the menu and then he called the waiter and placed the order. Whilst the meal was being prepared, he gave Denise the pictures. There were three; one of her sitting on the promenade wall with her legs crossed, and two of her standing in her garden where she lived. As she looked at all three, her mind went back over all those years ago. Then she looked at Glen and he said "Can I have one of those photographs?"

"Yes of course. Which one would you like?"

And he said, "I think the one of you in your garden standing by the rose bushes."

She gave it to him.

By this time their food was placed in front of them, and as they enjoyed their food, their conversation was pleasant and thoughtful.

When the evening came to a close, they had learned a great deal about each other, and it only remained for Glen to see Denise home.

As they stood at her front gate, he held her hand and said "I hope we will meet again?"

She looked firmly into his eyes and answered "Thanks for a lovely meal and evening. You have my phone number — you have only to ring me."

He then let go of her hand and said "Good night Denise, and thanks a lot. I am glad we have met and that I have told you everything."

The family wanted to know what sort of an evening she had, and all she said was "Marvellous" and as it was getting late she was soon off to bed. As she lay in bed, she thought of Glen. What did she think of him? He was a very attractive fellow. He had thick dark hair and his eyes were brown. His mouth was soft, and his face was slim with smiling eyes — not at all deceitful. He was tall and slim. His hands were soft. There was nothing objectionable about him. He had good manners and he was about her age. The chemicals between them were perfect. Only time itself would tell if a romance would be born.

A few weeks went by and Denise had concentrated on her business which now had all the hallmarks of success. As for Glen, his work as an engineer had taken him to London, but now he was on his way home to Preston and it was whilst sitting on the train that his thoughts were really concentrated on Denise — so much so, that he was determined to phone her for a date.

It was rather strange, because the very evening that he

phoned around 9 o'clock, the family had been talking about him, because it was soon to be Denise's birthday, the 10th September, and she would be twenty-eight years old, and the year — 1950.

Denise picked up the phone and Glen said "Is that you Denise?"

"Yes" she said.

"It's me Glen. I am phoning to ask you will you have dinner with me tomorrow evening? I have just returned from London on business where I have been since we last met."

Denise was overjoyed and said "Of course I will."

"Then shall we say I will pick you up at seven?"

"I look forward to it" said Denise.

She then returned to the lounge.

They all stared at her and said "Well?"

She smiled and said "That was Glen. He wants to take me out for a meal tomorrow night."

Then Mary said "Well?"

"What do you mean well?"

Mary said "Are you going?"

"Of course I am going." Denise looked at all of them and said "Alright, I am interested in him, and if it's successful I will be asking him home to meet you all. Now does that satisfy you?"

They all smiled, then her dad said, "I have not said a word, but I am looking forward to meeting him dear."

The following evening arrived, and Denise was very excited. It all seemed a long time ago since she had romance in her heart. It was their second date and both seemed very happy to be together.

Once inside the restaurant, Glen could not take his eyes off Denise.

The waiter stood aside knowing that they both had much to say. It was Glen who said "You know Denise, you really are a very beautiful and attractive young lady."

Denise said "Both my parents want me to take you home and meet you."

"That's funny, my parents want to meet you also" Glen said.

At that moment, the waiter came to their table and said "Are you ready to order Sir?"

Both Glen and Denise made their choice of food and it was during the meal and drinking the wine that Glen said "You know Denise, I know it's early days, but I must tell you that I have fallen in love with you."

Denise first looked down at the table, then she raised her head and looked straight at Glen and said, "I must confess, I feel the same way about you."

It was obvious that they had given the matter a great deal of thought. Then Glen said "Let me tell you this, I am sure I will get a divorce from Ruth, and we can then get married — that is if you wish to do the same? It's just a matter of time and paperwork."

"I hope so, because I would like this romance of our to develop into something permanent."

"Then so it shall darling," said Glen.

As the romance between Denise and Glen was beginning to take shape over the following weeks, it was Ruth's affair with Barry Thompson which was having its problems. Barry had promised Ruth that he would divorce his wife and marry her. They had of course had a great deal of intimate sex over the past years; but whenever the subject of him divorcing his wife came up, he made the excuse that he had to pick the right time because he had to consider the children — one boy of eleven and a girl of fourteen.

It was during a summer evening while Ruth and Barry were dining out in their usual restaurant that Ruth approached him again regarding him getting the wheels in motion for a divorce.

Ruth said "Don't you think you ought to tell your wife Sybil about us, and that you wish to get a divorce in order to marry me before she and the children go to your home in the South of France?"

Barry looked concerned. He sighed again and again. He fumbled with his wineglass. He ran his fingers through his hair. Then he said "Look Ruth, I have to pick the right time, and the time is not now."

Ruth was furious for she had been down this path many times. Then with an outraged look she said "Tell me truthfully, have you any intention of telling your wife or are you having me on? Because if so, you will regret it."

He looked at her with a serious glare, "Are you threatening me?" he said.

"You could say that" she said.

He looked her straight in the eye and said "I'm not used to being threatened, certainly not by a slut like you, and after all you were eager to go to bed with me. Who else would you bed down with after we got married?" She was now furious, for she now realised that no way was he going to divorce Sybil. "So that's it," she said.

"Yes, you could say that."

Ruth said, "Are you saying that you will not divorce Sybil?"

"That's exactly what I am saying, and if you ever thought I would, you must have been a bigger fool than I thought you were."

Silence was experienced across the dining table just as the waiter came up and said "Everything to your satisfaction Sir?"

Barry looked at the waiter and said "Yes, everything thank you."

Ruth collected her thoughts and looked Barry straight in the eye and said quietly "You'll live to regret what you have just said, you pig."

She then quietly got up from the table and left the restaurant, where outside she called a taxi, and in total silence she made her way home, where she sat down and thought out clearly what she should do.

## CHAPTER 9

After a few days had passed, and with a clear mind, and knowing that his wife had gone to France, she made her way to his office car park. She knew what time he would be leaving, so patiently she waited. Then out he came with one of his colleagues.

She walked towards them and said with a smile on her face "Hello Barry, can I cadge a lift?"

What could he do but say "OK". The colleague, like many others, was aware of their affair, and the last thing that Barry wanted was a scene.

So once in the car Barry said, "What's the meaning of this? I thought the other evening decided our future?"

She smiled and said "Oh Barry, you made me so mad. Please forgive me. I knew for sometime that you would not divorce Sybil, but I just hoped that if I made my point very clear you just might have come around to my way of thinking."

"Are you saying that if I don't get a divorce you don't mind if we continue our affair?"

"That's what I am saying Barry. You see I just can't live without you, and there is always hope that you might change your mind and divorce Sybil."

He stopped the car and put his arms around her he gave her a kiss and said "Look, the wife and the kids have gone to France, so why not come in for a drink?"

"That would be nice, but let us spend tomorrow evening in our favourite restaurant where it all began. I will come in my car first to your house, and I will dress appropriately for ending a lovely evening. I can then stay late and drive myself home. I will make it an evening to remember, if you know what I mean?"

"Oh I do darling. I will look forward to it."

She fell into his arms and kissed him by pushing her tongue into his mouth.

He then said "I can hardly wait."

When back in her flat she prepared herself for what had to be done the next evening.

It was an evening to be remembered — after all, it was Friday the 13th, and she was dressed for the kill. She wore a well-off-the-shoulder slimline colourful dress. Her hair hung low on her shoulders. She wore high heels — no tights, just knickers. She wore small earrings, a bracelet and a watch. Her nails were long and painted red. Her brown eyes matched her brown hair. Her eyelids were painted a pale shade of green. She really did look a temptress.

She was calm as she made her way to her car, for this was to be the night of revenge that she had planned down to the last detail of how to commit the perfect murder, and if as she thought, he did not suspect anything, then it *will* be the perfect murder. She was relying on his vanity. But who was to take the blame? Or had she arranged even that detail — we shall see?

She pulled off the road and into the drive through a brick pier entrance gate, and within moments she stopped the car at the front door. She then got out and adjusted her sexy dress. She pressed the door bell and Barry was there to let her in. The house was well sheltered by heavy trees. He pulled her into his arms and closed the door. He then kissed her as he ran his hands down her back and into the cheeks of her bottom. As he pulled his fingers into her bottom, she closed her cheeks which gripped his fingers. The front of him pressed hard against her breasts and stomach. It was obvious that from the start the evening was going to end up with intercourse on the bed completely naked.

They walked into the lounge, with his arm around her waist. The time was 7 o'clock so the evening was young.

He said "What do you want to drink?"

With a great deal of thought she then said "Oh make mine the usual cream sherry."

Whilst he was seeing to the drinks she was surveying the room and its contents. She then asked him "Have you heard from your wife?"

"Yes, and she is going to call this evening because one of the children has caught a bug and he has been sick."

Just at the moment the phone rang. He picked up the receiver "Hello Sybil" — there was a pause then he said "Oh thank God he has seen the doctor and he is much better. Oh that's marvellous" — another pause then he said "I'm glad you phoned early because I have a spot of work to do and I will not be going to bed late. Oh no, I'm not going out anyway so be good and take care. I will phone you tomorrow evening. God bless you darling." He then replaced the receiver and picked up his drink and walked over to Ruth. As he walked towards Ruth he said "Well are we going to waste time?"

Ruth walked towards him. She put her arms around him and said "Shall we repeat what we did at the door and then go to bed?"

His arms went from her shoulders down her back to her bottom where his fingers fondled her backside. He closed his eyes. He was miles away in thought and was captivated by her sexy figure and slimline frock. As she pushed her stomach against him, his leg slipped between hers as she slowly opened them. She pushed her lips against his and opened her mouth. Her tongue then slipped into his mouth. They both gave a sigh of emotion and affection, but what he did not know was in her hand she held a knife. She then with all her might plunged it into his back at the top of his neck. His eyes opened wide. He released his hold on her and tried to grab the knife in his back as he took a deep breath and painfully screamed out. She then pulled the knife out, and as he staggered backwards away from her, she plunged the blood-stained knife into his heart — not once, but twice. He fell helplessly forward. She stepped quickly aside as he fell face down on the floor. He was still breathing and then his body went limp. She wondered if she should stab him again, but decided to roll him over and look him in the face. She could see that he was dead. His eyes were wide open. His heart had stopped beating. His pulse had ceased to beat. She stood motionless looking at him. She then spent time wiping certain items clean that she may have handled. She then calmly undid the front door, and walked to her car.

She sat in the car for a moment. Then she switched on the ignition. She then took a deep breath and began to realise the serious side of what she had just committed, and so in her haste she drove rather quickly out of the drive through the brick piers and turned sharply left into the road, almost colliding with another car. What she did notice was that there was no one in the road watching her at the time. Soon she turned off the road towards where she lived. The car that followed her, carried straight on. So there was nothing for him to suspect.

Upon her arrival back home, she promptly made a pot of tea and relaxed in an armchair. She then had a great idea. She thought she would phone Denise, for this would give her an alibi.

Denise answered "Hello Ruth, how are you?"

Within seconds Ruth said "Oh I'm fine. I've been sitting here all evening and I thought why don't I give you a call."

"That's kind of you."

Then Ruth said "How are you and Glen getting on? He told me all about you and him. By the way is he with you at the moment, and have I interrupted anything?"

"No, he is not here, and how are you and Barry these days?" asked Denise.

"Just fine. We have recently been discussing about him getting a divorce from Sybil."

"So it's still on for you to marry him?" said Denise.

"Oh yes, it just takes a little time and he wants to pick the right moment to approach the delicate situation."

The conversation went on and on until Denise said "Well Ruth, I have a spot of ironing to do so I will say cheerio for now."

Denise then replaced the receiver and joined her mother.

Her mother said "Who was that dear?"

"Oh it was Ruth."

Then her mother said "Is there anything wrong dear?"

"No Mum, why do you say that?"

"Well dear, you looked a little puzzled."

Then Denise said "Well if you must know, I did think the phone call was a bit pointless. I realise that Glen has told her that I now know all about Barry, and she may think that I and Glen are very friendly, but somehow she was trying to tell me something."

Then her mother said "In what way dear?"

"Well she made a point of what time it was."

Her mother then said "I see what you mean."

Denise said "Oh well, I'll just get on with my ironing."

As for Ruth, she had much on her mind, such as the murder that she had just committed. She walked around her apartment, and grabbed the gin bottle. She drank only a little, then she sat down, and after many thoughts she decided to go to bed.

That evening, Sybil thought she would telephone Barry again from France, mainly because the next day she intended to take the children to visit an old friend, but she could not remember the address and she knew Barry would remember, and knowing that he was not going out, she thought 'Why not phone him?' She dialled several times, but naturally got no reply. She thought that he was either having a bath, or that he had gone out after all, so she left it for some time. In fact, it was after the children had gone to bed and it was now late and she tried many times, but finally she retired to bed and decided to phone him first thing in the morning. This she did, but there was no reply. She was of course now concerned. She then thought to phone his office around 10 o'clock.

When she made her call, she was informed that he had not turned up at the office. This was completely out of character regarding Barry, so she tried just after lunch time and spoke to a close colleague of Barry's, who was Harry Thorpe, she knew him very well. She said "Harry, I understand that Barry has not been in his office so far."

"That's right Sybil. I for one don't understand what could have happened to him. It's not like him not to phone in and tell us what's happening."

Sybil then said "Harry do you think you could pop round

home later and phone me?''

"Yes of course Sybil, no problem, I will be in touch. I have your phone number.''

The children then joined Sybil and asked "Is Daddy alright?''

She said "Yes of course dears. He has just got caught up on some business'' was all she could think of to say.

Around about five-thirty, Harry told his wife, "Look darling, I am going round to Barry's house. We are all puzzled as to what has happened to him today.''

"OK dear, I'll see you later.''

During the journey to Barry's house, Harry was trying to think why Barry had not contacted the office. However in no time at all Harry was driving into Barry's driveway. He came to a stop, got out of the car and walked to the front door. He pressed the door bell again and again. There was no answer. Even Harry now became very suspicious. He started to walk around the house and found nothing disturbed or suspicious. He looked through the windows but could see nothing. He then wondered was Barry ill in bed? The only way to find out was to go to the police station. So off he went as quickly as possible.

He walked straight up to the desk where a police officer said "You look worried Sir. Is there something wrong?''

"I'm not sure Officer.''

The policeman then said "Well Sir, perhaps you had better take your time and explain what's on your mind.''

Harry then went into details regarding the phone call from Sybil in France and to Barry's absence in the office and to the fact that he had been to his house.

The officer then said, "Well Sir, there is probably a perfect answer to it all. So without further delay, can I have details such as your name and address, also of your colleague?''

"Certainly Officer'' said Harry.

After a few moments the officer said "Right Sir, will you please take a seat and if you wish to make a phone call to your wife to let her know what is happening there is a public call box just over there.''

"Thank you I will phone my wife.''

Just as Harry came off the phone a plain-clothes gentleman approached him and said "Well Sir, shall we pop along to your friend's house!"

As they both walked out, they were met by another man. The plain-clothes officer then said "Oh this gentleman is a locksmith — just in case we have to make an entry." Harry gave instruction to the quickest way, and upon their arrival they still had no reply when they pressed the door bell.

The police officer strolled around the property and looked into several windows. The rooms were difficult to see into because of flowerbeds, and most rooms contained heavy furniture so it was suggested that the locksmith do his best. Within moments the front door was opened and they all went into the hall. The stairway was on the right, but the plain-clothes policeman pushed open the door on the left which was partly opened and he walked in — which was of course the lounge.

The others followed and there in the middle of the room they saw Barry on the floor. It was difficult to see him from any window because he had fallen between two large settees. A pool of blood was visible on the oatmeal-coloured carpet. He was on his back. His eyes were staring towards the ceiling. Poor Harry felt sick and the locksmith turned his head and walked away and gazed out of the window.

Harry then said "What now?"

The detective immediately phoned the station and put the wheels in motion for a murder case. He then told both men "Don't touch anything. In fact, I suggest that when the police arrive you had best return to your homes."

Within moments three police cars arrived with one containing Chief Detective Inspector Jim Ross and Sergeant Peter Webb. The inspector was a tall well-built man with dark hair and a few grey hairs. His sergeant was smartly dressed, but rather young with fair hair and full in the face. He looked a little cheeky and was quick to answer back. The inspector made straight for the body whereas the sergeant was quick to look at the windows for a break-in, whilst other police officers looked around outside.

Before Harry left, he discussed the matter with the inspector regarding Sybil the wife of Barry and he said "We will be contacting Mrs Thompson.''

Harry was pleased that he would not have the task of telling Sybil as to what had happened.

On their way back to the station Sergeant Webb said ''This could be your last case sir, as you are so close to retirement.''

''You could say that Webb.''

Then the sergeant said ''Well sir, what do you think?''

Ross then said ''When we are back at the station let's look at the facts as we have them.''

It was Webb who said ''Looking at the house sir, I would not think that they were short of money.''

''You're right Webb. We will have to look carefully at all the facts.''

The following day they visited Barry's company where he worked. They approached the reception desk.

It was Webb who said ''Good morning can we see your office manager?''

The receptionist then asked ''Have you got an appointment?''

''I'm afraid not,'' said Webb.

''Then who shall I say wants him, only he is rather busy?''

Webb then showed her his identity and said ''We are police officers.''

''One moment sir,'' she said. Then she rang through to the manager's office. ''Oh Helen, is Mr Taylor free, only I have two police officers here who wish to speak with him?'' There was a pause then the receptionist said ''Someone will be down right away.''

''Thank you,'' said Webb.

As the two officers stood aimlessly around, they were approached by a very attractive young lady who said ''Would you come this way please.'' She took them along a corridor and into the manager's room.

The manager said ''Good morning. My name is Taylor. Please be seated.'' As they both sat down he then said, ''Well gentlemen, I understand you are police officers. How can I help you?''

Then Ross said ''I am Chief Detective Inspector Ross and

this is Sergeant Webb. We are investigating the murder of one of your employees — a Mr Barry Thompson — and I wondered if you could answer a few questions. We would also like to interview members of your staff who were perhaps close to him in order to get some feeling as to who may have had a reason to murder him. I am not suggesting that anybody from here did murder him, but we have to start somewhere on our routine enquiries whilst we are waiting for Mrs Thompson to return from France.''

Webb had pen and paper at the ready as the manager said ''Well if I can help in any way, please go ahead and ask any questions.''

Ross then said ''You must have known him yourself very well Mr Taylor? Can you tell me what was he really like?''

The manager took a deep breath and then said ''Well, he has been with this company for the past fifteen years. He has always been conscientious. He knew his job regarding the selling of our equipment. He was also a very friendly-natured person. I'm afraid I know nothing of his private life. I believe he had a happy marriage. He has two children I think. That's about all I can tell you inspector.''

Webb interrupted by saying ''Would you know of anyone in the company who may have wanted to harm him in any way, such as wanting his position?''

''I think not'' said the manager.

''Well do you think that we could talk with some of his close associates in the firm?''

The manager then suggested that they use the room that they always hold their monthly meetings in. He then called his secretary to arrange this.

''You have been very helpful'' Ross said.

They were both then taken from the office into a nearby room which had a long conference table, where they both sat and made themselves comfortable. Within moments the secretary brought in a fellow and introduced him to them. She then left the room.

During the course of the morning, they had interviewed many male and female staff. They had also been well looked after with coffee. But now came the time to see the manager. Once again it was then that they thanked him for his co-operation, and they finally left.

It was during their lunch that Webb said "Well sir, what did you make of that lot?"

Ross then said "From my experience I would not think any of them appeared suspicious, but I did gather, despite what Mr Taylor said about Thompson's marriage, I think he was a bit of a ladies' man."

The sergeant put tongue in cheek and said, "I gathered that myself, sir, but I would not think that he had had any affairs with any of the fellows' wives."

"No Webb, but I did gather there was a person who was having an affair with him outside the company."

In the afternoon they were back in the police station and also they returned to the scene of the crime. Once inside they both went over the details that they had gathered from their previous investigation and whilst looking out of the window Ross said, "Tomorrow, Mrs Thompson returns to England and we shall be interviewing her."

Webb then said, "Well sir, there was no false entry. Whoever killed him, he was expecting that person, and judging by the way he was murdered surely only a man would have been that strong to have overpowered him. After all it did not appear as though there was much of a struggle."

"You're right, Webb, but it all seems too neat for me at this moment in time. However perhaps we shall see it all in a different light when we interview Mrs Thompson tomorrow, so let's call it a day, shall we?"

"A good idea, sir," said the sergeant.

The next day they went to Mrs Thompson's house. The police cars arrived at the front door and Mrs Thompson opened the door to let in the inspector, the sergeant and two other police officers — one of which was a female police constable. Mrs Thompson's expression on her face was one that you would have expected of a person whose husband had just been murdered when she was not even in England at the time the crime was committed.

The inspector said, "I am aware of the shock that all this must have been to you Mrs Thompson, and I will make my necessary enquiries as brief and as painless as possible. It is however obvious that someone or somebodies wished your husband out of the way. I can tell you this, that we have interviewed several of the staff where he worked, so perhaps you can tell me what you know or think about this terrible crime.''

He paused and the sergeant said, ''What we do know, Mrs Thompson, is that whoever killed him, he must have let them in so we have to suspect that the killer knew your husband and perhaps your husband was expecting someone that evening around 7 o'clock. We have enough evidence to know that he died between seven and eight.''

She then said, ''Well I phoned him and spoke with him just after seven. He told me he had some work to do and would not be going out at all. He seemed perfectly happy — his voice gave this impression — he asked if I was alright, also the children. I told him our son was much better and he was pleased to hear this.''

Then the inspector interrupted her and said, ''Tell me, have you any idea of any person who would wish to do this kind of thing to your husband?''

She then said, ''I have no idea, Inspector.''

Then the inspector said, ''I must ask you this, was there another woman in his life?''

She took her time, then she looked at the inspector and said, ''Yes Inspector, my husband did have affairs with other women, but I always shut a blind eye to it all for the children's sake and I knew that every affair was always short-lived.''

The sergeant got up from his chair and looked straight at Mrs Thompson and said, ''What made you so confident that he would never leave you regardless as to how much he desired another woman?''

''Well, Sergeant, I have all the money. I have my own private income which is very substantial. Barry's wages were not bad, but not all that great, and he loved to spend money. I was always gracious on money matters for I knew this was the way to keep him.''

Then the inspector asked, ''Tell me would you know the name of his current affair?'' She wondered whether to answer this but the inspector said, "If you give us this information it may help us to find your husband's killer. I must remind you that withholding valuable information is a crime."

She then said, "Yes I realise that and I do know the name of who was his latest woman friend. Her name is Mrs Ruth Gould and I have her address and telephone number."

"Tell me, how did you come by knowing this, Mrs Thompson?" said the sergeant.

"Well, I wanted a couple of his suits cleaned and so before taking them to the dry-cleaners I naturally went through his pockets and I found a piece of crumpled-up paper. I was about to throw it in the bin, but I was curious in case it was something he wanted to keep, so I unravelled it and saw in his own handwriting her name and phone number. I then got hold of the telephone book and found out where she lived. I made a note of it and then destroyed his piece of paper. I did not approach him about this as I have already said I was always aware of his affairs."

"That's very interesting," said the inspector. He then asked her, "Tell me, how long would you say that this particular affair had been going on?"

She then took her time and said "It's funny you should ask that."

"Why, Mrs Thompson?" said the sergeant.

"Well, I think for a very long time. You see, that particular suit he had not worn for a very long time; maybe a year or so. The paper did look discoloured and thinking about it I think he had an affair with someone else during that time."

"What you are saying is that this particular person might have thought she was his only affair, but he was also unfaithful to her and she did not know it," said the inspector. "Well, Mrs Thompson, you have been most helpful and I think we have now all that we need to know from you for the time being. If we need you, you will be available — that is, you are not planning to return to France in the near future?"

"That's right, Inspector," she said.

The inspector and his staff then made their way back to the police station.

It was at the police station that Ross said to his sergeant, "I think we should call upon and question this Mrs Ruth Gould."

"Shall we go now sir?" said Webb.

"Why not?" said Ross.

During their journey, Webb said, "Have you anything in particular that you will be asking her, sir?"

"Not really — look out Webb, we have gone past the street," the inspector said.

Then Webb said, "Sorry sir, I was not thinking. By the way sir, if she is not there, what do we do?"

"What do you mean 'what do we do'? We leave a note in her door and we phone later." By this time they had arrived outside her apartment.

"This looks like a nice neighbourhood," said the sergeant.

"Well, get out Webb, or are you going to sit here all day?" said Ross. They both approached the main entrance and the inspector said, "Well Webb, press the bell."

"Oh yes, sir."

A voice was then heard — "Who is it?"

"Is that Mrs Gould?" said the sergeant.

"Yes, who is that?"

Webb looked at his inspector and said, "It's the police, Mrs Gould. Can we come up?"

She then answered "The door is open."

They then proceeded up the stairs and on their approach to the apartment they noticed that the door was open.

Upon entering Mrs Gould said, "I'm Mrs Gould. Do come in."

They walked in and noticed that the apartment was very well furnished. It was all in good taste.

She then said, "Do sit down. Can I offer you both a drink or would you prefer tea?"

"No, nothing at the moment. We won't take up much of your time. I am Chief Detective Inspector Ross, and this is Sergeant Webb."

"What can I do for you, gentlemen?"

Ross then opened up the conversation by saying, "A Mr Barry Thompson has been found murdered. You may have read all about it in the national press."

She butted in by saying "Yes, but what has that got to do with me?"

Ross then continued by saying, "By the way you have a very nice apartment here, it must cost quite a lot of money to keep up?"

"I manage, but I'm sure you have not come here to discuss the upkeep of my apartment."

"No, you are right, Mrs Gould. We understand you were familiar with the deceased."

She looked straight at Ross as she sat in a very comfortable armchair and said, "Well, I have met him."

"We have been given to understand that you were on intimate terms with the gentleman."

She looked alarmed — in fact she looked furious — and replied, "I don't know what you mean!"

The sergeant then said, "Well, we have conclusive evidence that you were in love with him, and he with you. In fact it had been planned for him to divorce his wife and to marry you. Do you deny this?"

She gave out a sigh. She then stood up and strolled across the room. She then turned and faced the inspector and said, "Alright, it's true we were in love with each other and he was planning to tell his wife when she returned from France that he wanted a divorce."

"And you believed that?" said the sergeant.

She looked at him and said, "I had no reason not to believe him."

"Tell me," said the inspector, "I take it that your husband was aware of your affair and of your intention of asking for a divorce to marry Mr Thompson?"

"Yes, he knew all about it. I made no secret of what I intended to do."

The inspector then said, "Tell me Mrs Gould, I assume this apartment and most, if not all, of its luxuries were provided by the late Mr Thompson?"

The inspector's remark took her by surprise and she said, "What has that got to do with you? That is my private life, and what is more I would hardly want to murder the man who provided me with all this."

"That is true, but if he did not intend to divorce his wife

surely your lifestyle would change sooner or later?'' said the inspector.

She uttered not a word. She just stood motionless.

''Well, Mrs Gould you have not answered the inspector's question,'' said the sergeant.

''I see it's of no importance,'' said Mrs Gould.

The sergeant then said, ''Tell me, Mrs Gould, it seems that your husband had no objection to your wanting a divorce and marrying again?''

She again did not answer.

Then the inspector said ''Did your husband know Mr Thompson?''

''Yes, they had met on a couple of occasions at a party.''

Then the sergeant said, ''It would appear that your husband was a very placid and understanding person.''

She collected her thoughts then said, ''Well, I would not go as far to say that.''

''What do you mean?'' asked the inspector.

''Well, he has always been in love with me to the point of being possessive and rather jealous.''

''I see, Mrs Gould, and I thank you for being so helpful. We will be in touch if we need you for further questioning. We will see ourselves out. Good day!''

The inspector stopped at the door, in fact the sergeant bumped into him.

''Sorry, sir!''

''That's alright, Webb'' said the inspector as he turned and walked back into the room. He saw her pouring out a drink for herself.

She turned and said, ''I thought you had gone, Inspector.''

''I'm sorry, but I overlooked asking you where were you on the night of the crime?''

It took her by surprise, but the sergeant was not, because his boss was known for doing this sort of thing.

She fumbled for words, she was definitely taken off her guard in fact she was shattered and said, ''Can I offer you both a drink?''

''No thank you, just answer my question will you?''

She puffed and sighed, her hand shook a little and she spilt her drink, then she said, "Ah, I was in all evening, that's right, now I remember. I did not go anywhere."

The sergeant who by now was back in the room said, "Is there anyone who can confirm that you spent the evening on your own, like was there someone with you?"

Again she was searching for words, then she said, "I was on my own." Then she said as though she had planned the answer should she be asked "Oh I did make a phone call to my dear friend, Denise Povey. We talked for some time. You know what women are like when they start talking."

"About what time was that?" asked the sergeant.

It was obvious she had made such a call intentionally for she swiftly said, "Oh, sometime between 6.30 and 7.30."

"Thank you, we will get this confirmed with Denise Povey. Thanks again for your co-operation."

As they were driving away the sergeant said, "Well sir, what do you make of that?"

"Well Webb, I need to meet her husband and Miss Denise Povey."

Back at the station, and whilst drinking a cup of tea, the sergeant said, "Well sir, since none of Mr Thompson's colleagues at work are under suspicion and his wife knows of no person wishing to harm him, could it not be a case of a jealous husband after all? She did say they had met on more than one occasion, and surely if her husband had phoned the deceased that evening, either on a friendly basis or to discuss his co-operation in agreeing to a divorce or something — after all we do know that whoever did it did not have to force their way in — and perhaps he took a knife? She did say he was also the jealous type, and so the deceased may have agreed to meet him on a friendly basis. Who knows?"

The inspector then said, "What you say makes sense Webb, but it all seems too easy. As for me there is something about Mrs Gould that makes me think that she is greedy, and anything but a pleasant person. However, let's wait and see when we meet Mr Gould what alibi he has for that evening."

"If he has not got an alibi sir, do we pull him in on suspicion?" said the sergeant.

"Well, probably," said the inspector.

With the day now behind them and thinking of all the

information that they had collected, they knew that they had a lot more groundwork to do.

The next day was wet and windy as they drove to Mr Gould's house. The house was situated on an estate of modern houses all looking much the same. It was not an executive area — quite the opposite to Mr Thompson's house. They knocked on the door and Mr Gould opened it. They explained who they were and the nature of their business.

He invited them in, and they sat in the small lounge. "Can I offer you a cup of tea or coffee?"

"No thank you," said the inspector. "I will come straight to the point. This routine enquiry is about a Mr Thompson who was found murdered about a week ago, and I would like to ask you a few questions," said the inspector.

"Yes, of course, Inspector."

"Tell me, Mr Gould, how well did you know Mr Thompson?"

Glen was very relaxed as he had nothing to hide, but he was concerned as to the seriousness of these enquiries. "Well, Inspector, I met the chap on two occasions. His company and mine did business with each other, so it's not surprising that at some time a party was given by one of the companies. So members of each company were able to meet."

"I understand that wives are also invited?"

"Yes, that is so."

Then the sergeant said, "Tell me Mr Gould, were you aware that your wife was having an affair with Mr Thompson at the time of some of these parties?"

Glen knew that this kind of question would come up, so he was prepared to answer it promptly and said, "Yes, I must admit I did observe their familiarity."

The inspector then said, "Tell me, did it worry you?"

"Yes, it did at first, in fact enough for me to want to harm him just to try and stop the affair before it got too strong."

Then the sergeant said, "In fact, strong enough for you to want to kill him?"

"No Sergeant, I have a certain amount of jealousy in my nature, especially as I look like losing the one I love, but to kill — oh no, never that, I would not know how to kill."

The inspector then said, "Tell me, where were you on the night of the murder?"

"Well, Inspector, it happened to be the night that I was entirely on my own."

"What do you normally do with your evenings?" said the sergeant.

"I play billiards two nights a week in the local billiard hall, but that particular night I stayed in. Ah no, I did go out for a walk. I sometimes do this. I enjoy walking if the evening is a pleasant one and I have little else to do."

"Did you see anyone in your travels, and what time would that be?"

Then Glen answered, "Oh, any time between seven and eight."

The sergeant then said, "Where do you usually take your walk?"

With raised eyebrows, Glen said, "I usually stroll along the canal. I often see fellows fishing along the bank."

"Did any of them see you?" asked the sergeant.

"Not that I know of," said Glen.

"Well, Mr Gould, thank you for your help. You will be hearing from us," said the inspector. They were then shown out of the house and they returned to the police station to report on their progress.

Naturally the local and national press wanted to know how the enquiries were going on, and of course were they any nearer to making an arrest? Well, it did look black for Glen. After all, he did have a motive, and it was possible he could have got in without breaking in, and he had no proof that he just spent the evening on his own. So after a great deal of thought back at the station they had no alternative but to visit Glen once more. This time there were two police cars and the press was around just in case there was an arrest.

As the cars pulled up outside Glen's house the public were also curious. The inspector and his sergeant made their way to the front door and Glen was seen letting them in.

The inspector faced Glen and said, "Mr Gould, I'm afraid I have to inform you that we are here to arrest you for the murder of Mr Thompson."

It took Glen back a bit. He was of course shocked. He then gathered some of his things and walked out of his house. The press took photographs. A lot of shouting went on as he was hastily pushed into a police car and was driven off to the local station where he spent the night in a cell, before being taken to London the next day.

Denise was, of course, shocked but Ruth was very calm. It was Denise's parents and sister who that evening discussed the whole thing, for no way were they going to believe that Glen was a murderer. But how the hell was he going to prove his innocence?

The next day Denise went round to Ruth's apartment, but Ruth did not want to see her. Denise insisted, so Ruth finally let her in and the two girls came face to face.

It was Denise who spoke first. "Ruth, you must know that Glen is not a murderer."

Ruth butted in and said, "Oh come off it Denise the police are right, they don't make those kind of mistakes. He murdered Barry because of his jealousy. He couldn't bear the thought of losing me. He has always been that way. Every time I have had other men, he often threatened to kill them."

"Oh come off it Ruth, often people in temper say things like that, it's just something to say. It does not mean when it comes to it that they will kill, and you know that." Denise was furious.

But Ruth was cool and very calm as she said "Is that all you have come round to see me about? I think you should leave, after all you might kill me now because you think I have spoilt your silly romance with Glen. He never loved you, and to prove it he even killed Barry because he could not have me."

With that Denise said, "Don't worry Ruth, I'm going, but Glen will get off, and the murderer will be found; after all, the murderer might even be you. I must admit that with my deepest revenge that I had during the war concerning Heidrick Von Steinrickter which would have been justified, I still did not stoop to murder and possibly jeopardize my mission; justice was done in that case and justice will be done in this case — you will see — I'm no fool Ruth." Denise then left leaving Ruth not so sure of herself as she wondered just what Denise might come up with.

That evening Denise discussed the whole affair with her family and of course at the stage of the murder enquiries, Denise was not involved.

It was her father who said "Something will turn up, I'm sure."

"I know he is innocent," said Denise.

Then her sister said "Let's face it, he is hardly likely to murder Barry, especially when he is in love with you Denise, and she wanted a divorce to marry Barry, and Glen wanted them to get married so that you and Glen could make something of your lives. I'm sure someone else wanted him dead, and that someone he knew very well."

Then her mother said "Would it help if you explained your situation with Glen to the police?"

Her father said "That's not a bad idea, but let's face it, he still has no alibi for that night, and you could not say that he was with you all evening. First of all it would be a lie, and they would ask why you and Glen had not mentioned it before, and they would know you are just saying that to protect him because of your love for him. It would not help him in any way. Oh no, we can only hope that something will turn up, but I think what your mother suggested was a good idea."

## CHAPTER 10

Denise could not settle down at all with her business now that Glen was in custody in London. The inspector and the sergeant were going over the details carefully with a fine-tooth comb. The sergeant thought it was a plain case of murder based on jealousy, but the inspector still thought differently. He just did not think that Glen had it in him to go that far and kill, and he still felt that Ruth was a cool and bitter woman.

However, appeals were put out on television and radio for anyone to come forward who may have seen Glen that evening — but unfortunately no one came forward — not until The News was shown on television. It was then that a milkman, who delivered milk at the Thompson house, went to the local police station and said to the desk sergeant "I would like to see someone concerning the murder of Mr Thompson."

He was then taken into the office of Inspector Ross. Within minutes both the inspector and his sergeant entered the office and the inspector then introduced himself and his sergeant.

When all were seated the inspector said "Now sir, perhaps you will be kind enough to explain why you are here?"

The milkman then said "I have come because of the appeal regarding the murder of a Mr Thompson. I don't know how important it is."

"Well sir, perhaps you had better take your time and tell the inspector all you know" said the sergeant.

The man then started by saying, "Well, the morning after the murder I went to the Thompson's house as usual to leave them their regular order of milk, and as I picked up the empty bottles, I found this on the doorstep." He then handed a very tiny earring to the inspector. It's colour was red.

Then the sergeant said, "Is that all you found?"

"Yes" the milkman said.

Then the sergeant said "What made you keep it?"

At that moment a cup of coffee was brought into the office for him to drink. He then said "Well sir, I took it home to my wife when I finished my rounds and I gave it to her, and I said 'look what I have found this morning, it's smaller than any of yours'."

The inspector said "What made you say that?"

"Well sir, my wife has earrings of all sizes, and she has always boasted of having the smallest earrings ever made."

"I see, but what made you keep it?" said the inspector.

"Well, the wife is like that. She will look around and try to find a smaller pair if I know her, that's just what she will do."

The interview then came to an end, and details were taken regarding the milkman for future reference.

The earring was kept for the time being, but it was not mentioned in any way. Also another piece of information was brought forward — it was a local motor mechanic who visited the police station — and once again both Ross and Webb saw him. His information was more important. Apparently Mrs Gould went to the garage where he worked to have her car serviced, and it was whilst it was being done that he noticed her offside wing had been damaged. He brought this to her attention and suggested that whilst her car was in for a service, they could repair it for her. She agreed to this, and so it was done. He himself saw no reason to report this, after all, repairs are going on all the time. But because of the appeal for people to come forward, it made him think, because a few days before her car came into his garage, he remembered driving with his wife along the road where the Thompsons lived, and somewhere along that road a car shot out of a driveway with undue care, and his wife said 'Look out darling'. He then carried on by saying "I put my foot on the brake which allowed the car to speed down the road in front of us. There were no other cars going up or down the road at that time. The only remark I made was 'women drivers'."

The sergeant then asked him "What day was that sir, and the time?"

He answered, "Strangely enough it was the night that a murder was committed somewhere in that road. I did not attach much importance to the incident until the request on the television."

He was then asked by the inspector "About what time was that?"

He then said "I would say it was around 8 o'clock, because my wife and I had planned to eat out that evening in a local restaurant, and we always eat around eight if we dine out."

All this information was very helpful, especially when another man came into the station and said "Can I see the inspector for a moment?"

Once again both Ross and Webb interviewed the man.

It was the inspector again who said "Well sir, what can you tell us that will help us with this murder case?"

He looked straight at Ross and said "Well Inspector, on the evening of the murder there was a gentleman walking along the canal, but not on the pathway. He must have been up on the grassy slope, because my old dog Jack is a soppy old dog, but he does not run to everybody. But as we were walking, he took off slowly but determined to go somewhere. He does this if he sees something moving in the long grass. I paid no attention to him, but for a moment he went out of sight. I got a little anxious and started to walk into the direction that he had taken; but at that moment I could see he was coming back, and I noticed a fellow between myself and the chaps fishing at the canal. He did not look my way, but I heard him say 'goodbye Jack'. First of all I thought he was someone who knew me and my dog Jack, but then I realised that as a stranger he must have made a fuss of my dog and looked at his name on his collar — that's all I can say."

The inspector thanked the man for coming forward, and after he had left, leaving his name and address, the inspector said "Well Webb, I think we are getting somewhere with all this information."

The inspector and his sergeant started to piece together the information they had at hand.

But in the meantime, Denise had decided to take a chance and at least tell the truth about her and Glen. So off she went to the local police station and explained her relationship with Glen. She told the inspector "I don't want to make things worse for Glen Gould, and I would rather our association not be made public, as I would not want the public to get the wrong idea about us both." So this information was kept confidential.

The next day, Inspector Ross called Webb into his office at 9 o'clock. He said "Sit down Webb. What I have been suspecting for some time may well come true."

Webb then said "This information that we have received will help prove Gould's innocence, but we still have not got the one who did the murder."

"That's where you may be wrong Webb," the inspector said.

"What do you mean sir?" said Webb.

The inspector then got up from his chair and looked out of the window. He took his time and then said, "If this information that we now have takes the pressure off Mr Gould, then we must release him immediately. It will then put the real murderer on his or her guard. So before we make any assumptions, why don't we first of all return to the Thompsons' house and see if there is any white paint on the brick pier of their driveway? And why don't we get a search warrant to search Mrs Gould's apartment for the other small earring? We know that finding her fingerprints won't help us, because we know, and so does Mrs Thompson know, that she had visited her house when she was away."

The sergeant then got up from his chair and said "You know sir, you have always suspected Mrs Gould. I don't know how you do it?"

"Just years of experience and dealing with human nature — that's all Webb."

The following morning, they both visited the Thompsons' house, and as they both got out of the police car, leaving the driver sitting in it, they made their way straight to the right-hand brick pier. When facing the house, and sure enough about a car wing height, there was white paint on the brickwork.

They had the police officer in the car call the station for photographs to be taken, and whilst they remained at the entrance it was the sergeant who said "Well sir, you are on the right track, sir."

"It seems that way Webb."

"What now sir?" Webb asked.

"After the photographer has been, we will return to the station for that search warrant of Mrs Gould's apartment."

Soon the police photographer arrived, and successful photographs were taken. The police then left the house, without contacting Mrs Thompson of course.

Back at the station, the police checked that Mrs Gould was at home. So they made their way to her apartment.

She let them in, and the police inspector said "Mrs Gould, I have a warrant to search your apartment. I hope you have no objections, unless you have something to hide?"

She looked amazed to say the least of it. "I have nothing to hide. But why do you need to search my apartment? Surely my husband is the obvious guilty person, and that is why you have charged him with the murder?"

The sergeant then said "Well Mrs Gould, it has looked that way and that's why we took him in to custody for a period. As you know, we can not keep him in prison indefinitely."

"I understand that, but with the evidence that you have, I thought it was sufficient to charge him for the crime pending a court trial in London. So why search my apartment? If you tell me what you are looking for, I will be happy to get it for you."

The inspector then interrupted her by saying "To tell you the truth Mrs Gould, we have received information recently, which we have checked out to be true, which has put a new light on the case, and I'm happy to say we will be releasing your husband soon, as he is not the number one suspect. In fact I do not suspect him at all. I can tell you this, that I have not been too sure that he did commit murder, but with no alibi and what seemed to be a motive to kill, put him in a very difficult position to say the least of it."

By this time the police had made a thorough search, when suddenly an officer came out of the bedroom and into the lounge and said "Is this what you want sir?"

The inspector looked at what he had in his hand and said "Ah that is exactly what I want." The inspector turned towards Mrs Gould and said, "This is your earring is it not?"

She looked at it and said with caution, "It might be."

"Come off it Mrs Gould, you know it is and we have the other one which you lost on the night of the murder."

Then she said "There are many such earrings."

The inspector then said, "I think not, and you know it."

The sergeant then said to the police crew "OK fellows, we have what we came for." The police then started to make their way out. The sergeant stood next to the inspector and said "I am sorry Mrs Gould, but we have to ask you to come with us to the station. We need a statement from you regarding the murder of Mr Thompson."

She was furious. She walked from one side of the room to the other, and then said "I shall call my lawyer."

Then the sergeant said, "You can do that at the station."

She was then taken to the station where she was charged with the murder of Mr Thompson pending on recent information received from several witnesses. And that same day Glen Gould was released in the presence of his solicitor. It was now clear to the inspector that Ruth Gould murdered Barry Thompson, for he realised that she knew that Barry had no intentions of leaving his wife to marry her. She also knew that she had lost Glen and thought because all was lost why not kill Barry and throw the suspicion onto Glen. She had carefully made a point of telephoning Denise to prove that she was at least in her apartment and nowhere else, because she knew that if Denise phoned back she would be there. She also found out that Glen was not with Denise, for she wanted to be sure that he was on his own. She also knew that it was not unusual for him to take a stroll alone, and if this was so, then he would find it difficult to have an alibi. She set the trap by telling the police that Glen had met Barry, and so it would not be impossible for him to visit Barry for a general chat about her leaving him to marry Barry. And so it looked as though Glen, in a fit of jealousy, knifed Barry and killed him. It all seemed so easy. In fact it was because it looked so easy that the inspector had second thoughts. So he arrested Glen quickly to put Ruth off her guard, and to force witnesses to come forward.

The way Inspector Ross works, has always fascinated Sergeant Peter Webb. It was Webb who said to the inspector in a local pub "You know sir, I shall never be as good as you. I admire the way that you control your emotions. You give nothing away."

Then the inspector said "Oh I don't know Webb, I am sure there was a moment when you gave Mrs Gould a great deal of thought regarding the possibility of her being the murderer. I am sure that when your time comes for you to be in charge of such a case, you will know just what to do, and who to suspect as the guilty one."

With Glen now released from the charges against him, Ruth was taken into custody and charged with the murder of Barry Thompson, and with all the witnesses that came forward, and the evidence that the inspector and the sergeant gave at the trial, she finally confessed to having murdered Barry Thompson, and she was hung for this crime.

Denise and Glen were starting a new future as they strolled along the Blackpool seafront arm in arm. The Povey family was now one big happy family. As for Mrs Thompson, she eventually sold up her home and went home to France, where the children were educated.

## CHAPTER 11

A year had now passed since the trial of Ruth for the murder of Barry Thompson — all of which was now history — but the association between Denise and Glen had developed on a very serious nature, and it looked as though they could plan for a September wedding. Great excitement was now being experienced by her parents. Her father was also coming up for retirement, and her sister Mary had found herself a boyfriend with the intention of getting married.

Denise's shops were doing well, and her sister really enjoyed helping Denise to run them. Glen's parents were looking forward to his marriage, and it was whilst Denise and Glen were strolling along the promenade that Glen said "Let us sit down here dear." They sat for a moment, then Glen said, "You know dear, I hope that when you marry me you will not be bored."

"Bored?" said Denise.

"Yes bored. You see, I have not led a very exciting life as you dear for instance. You are a capable dancer, good enough to take on London theatres. You had the guts to take on the German Army, and of all your experiences in the SOE, to say nothing of your success in owning your own fashion shops. Look at me I'm just an engineer and I have nothing to show for it. What have I done?"

"Nonsense. I would not have anyone else, and I am looking forward to spending the rest of my life with you, and don't you forget it." She put her head on his shoulder and said "At least a great deal of good has come out of our struggle for survival, and there is Mrs Thompson now living in France, and I am sure she is glad to be well rid of her husband, and you and I can settle down with a clear conscience of doing no wrong. What we have to do is to plan our honeymoon and our home and where that will be.''

Glen cuddled her very tightly and said "For our honeymoon why don't we go to Corfu and see some of your old friends, unless it is too painful with memories? And so for our home. What about that nice new estate of executive type of buildings just outside of the town?''

Denise removed her head from his shoulder and said "You know you are not as dumb as you look. There could be too many painful memories returning to Corfu, how about Austria?''

With that they both got up and went arm in arm along the promenade.

A week or two went by, and it was suggested that both families met for a meal to celebrate the good news. They were all dressed up in their Sunday best and chose Denise's uncle's restaurant, which was of course a Greek restaurant. So during the meal, much Greek was spoken.

That night over dinner, Glen stood up and said, "Can I have all of your attention please, just to tell you that tomorrow Denise and I are going out to choose an engagement ring which we will celebrate the occasion here in this restaurant on Sunday night, and we will then tell you of the date that we shall get married.''

For a moment it was silent, then suddenly they all smiled and clapped and cheered just as her uncle came with one of the waiters and poured out champagne in their glasses. It really was a wonderful evening.

As planned, the next day both Denise and Glen went to a local jeweller's shop and carefully chose their engagement ring.

There and then in a little cafe, over a cup of tea, Glen put the ring on Denise's finger and said "This is our first commitment and the beginning of a wonderful courtship and romance for the rest of our lives.''

H

When Sunday evening arrived, it was a night to be remembered. Glen had arranged for everybody to start their meal with a glass of sherry, and at the point in time he stood up and said "Just to welcome you all to our engagement dinner, which is a milestone to our future together, and I can now tell you all that we have decided to marry on the 10th September — we plan to spend two weeks in Austria for our honeymoon."

Everybody was now so happy, and as the evening came to a close, both Glen and Denise just knew that they had done the right thing.

In the coming weeks, not only were the wedding plans made, but they had bought their house on the new estate, so that upon their return from their honeymoon in Austria, they could settle down to furnishing their home. Denise really felt that for the first time in her life that she was about to be repaid for everything that she had done in the past.

The wedding of the 10th September arrived. Denise made a beautiful blushing bride with her gorgeous blonde hair, and her trim figure dressed in white. Her sister was her maid of honour, and she was dressed in a peach-coloured dress and looking wonderful with her dark hair. Glen's best man was a workmate of his who was single and who lived with and looked after his ageing mother. His name was Roy. Both the groom and the best man were dressed in morning suits, carrying top hats. It really was a grand turn-out. As for the day, the sun was up early and shone bright all day. The reception was held in one of the local hotels. After the reception, and all the speeches were over, the bride and groom mingled with the guests. It was a very happy day — but it was time for the bride and groom to change into more casual dress as they prepared themselves to say goodbye.

Soon they were on their way to the airport by taxi where they stayed overnight in the airport hotel. It was of course to be their first night together as man and wife, and so it was the end of a perfect day.

The next day after breakfast, the taxi arrived and with

suitcases in their hands, they were soon on their way to the airport. Again the weather was just perfect, and as they walked towards the check-in counter, people just stared at Denise. She really did look like Doris Day. Glen was so proud to be with her, as they walked to the departure lounge, where they had coffee and bought papers to read on the journey. Soon the destination board indicated that their flight was ready for boarding, so up they got with other passengers and made their way to the awaiting aircraft. Once on board, they were soon cleared for takeoff. So down the runway the plane travelled, and soon they were flying at 30,000 feet, when lunch was served. They just could not take their eyes off each other. They could not believe what was happening to them; and so in no time at all, it was touch down in Vienna, and their honeymoon had started.

But now that Glen and Denise's life was just beginning, we ask what became of Wendy Dalter, whose humble holidays were spent in Blackpool where her friendship with Denise began, for she also paid a heavy price during the war — so let me continue with the life and times of Wendy Dalter.

*PART 2*

## CHAPTER 12

The year was 1920 and the month was November, it was bleak and fog shrouded the town of Croydon making travel very difficult. The autumn leaves had fallen, the local park deserted, the High Street stores had closed. Only a few people were making their way home. The time now was 9 o'clock in the evening.

In a terraced house in an average street where the buildings dated from the 19th century, a gas light was burning, for many such premises were not so fortunate as to have electricity laid on for lighting, and there in this rented house a baby was born — Wendy Dalter.

It was now just over two years since the First World War was over, a new beginning had begun for this little mortal. If you had passed that house you would have heard her first cry as she entered a new world. Her father, having served his country in the Army in France, was now employed as a bus driver on the General Buses. These were the days when the wheels were solid rubber and not filled with air so the ride was somewhat uncomfortable. There was, of course, the tram which gave you a smoother ride, but rather noisy.

Wendy's mother worked in a laundry and her duties meant that she did a great deal of ironing. The work was hard with a steam iron; the hours were long and the pay was just a few shillings a week. She had a hard time giving birth to Wendy, so much so that the doctor told her that she could never have any more children. So Wendy became the only child. She was very plain for a baby with no hope of having outstanding features, but both her mother and father adored her.

With Christmas now behind them and the new year passing by, Wendy showed signs of having a wonderful nature, which was to be her hallmark for the future years to come. As a schoolgirl she lacked the possibility of becoming academic, but showed great signs of being very practicable. She excelled in initiative among her school friends, and being a quiet girl she remained close to her mother. At the age of fifteen she left school and worked in the local store as an assistant on the cosmetic counter. The little money she earned helped her parents whose own earnings were very little, to say the least of it.

Two years later, at the age of seventeen, she decided to spend a holiday without her parents but with her Blackpool friend Denise Povey. For two weeks she stayed at her home and enjoyed the bright lights of Blackpool and spent several evenings at the local dance hall. They were much admired by many fellows but romance was not on their minds; all they wanted to do was to enjoy swimming during the day and strolling along the promenade. They also talked about all the holidays that they had spent together since 1928 when she and her parents first went to Blackpool. Now as a teenager her hair settled comfortably on her shoulders, and having worked in cosmetics since leaving school, she became very attractive. With all this going for her she had no desires for running with the pack and flirting with the boys.

Her father was a gentle man and had done well on the buses, for he was now a bus inspector. Her mother who no longer worked long hours in the laundry, but stayed at home to keep things ticking over, had unfortunately developed breast cancer and so the future did not look good. Both her parents were devoted to each other which made a very happy family. Wendy's only interest was she wanted to learn how to ice skate. There were two ice rinks close to her home — one was in Streatham and the other in Purley, and both her parents encouraged her desire to skate. So every Wednesday and Friday evening they would all go skating. Her parents were hopeless, but Wendy was a natural — but they all got a great deal of fun out of it.

As the years got close to 1939, the Second World War looked inevitable. Adolf Hitler was now a very powerful leader and the threat to Europe with his demands gave great worry to countries on the borders of Germany. Diplomatic relations between England and Germany failed miserably as Adolf Hitler thumped the table and demanded expansion for The Fatherland. So in order to compromise with him, Czechoslovakia was sacrificed and given to him without a shot being fired. It gave him the assurance that both England and France were weak, but it gave England a chance to prepare production for war, and so between 1938 and 1939 England had a breathing space.

Life for Wendy had its sad moments because on the 3rd of August, 1939 her mother was rushed into the Croydon General Hospital to undergo an emergency operation for cancer — but all was lost, she died. It was a blow that shook Wendy terribly. She thought it was the end, but life must go on. They buried her mother in the local cemetery.

The following month Germany marched into Poland, and so the Second World War had begun. Wendy was now a very attractive young lady at the age of nineteen. A very quiet Christmas was spent with her father and in no time at all they entered 1940. A new life and new adventures were about to begin.

Tragedy struck again in 1940. When her father was at work at the bus depot — German bombers must have mistaken the bus depot for a military target. The raiders dropped a string of delayed action bombs at a low altitude, and before he and other staff could run for cover, the bombs exploded killing her father and several others. Wendy was now all on her own. In no time at all it had made her a rather hard person, so much so that it was not long before she gave in her notice, and volunteered for the Forces and joined the medical service. It was so unlike her, but perhaps she felt she could save life, having lost her mother and father. So into training she went and became a very good nurse. She looked very attractive in her uniform and having led a very serious life it obviously helped her to gain the confidence of her superiors. When the time came that she qualified as a nurse, she took the whole job very seriously.

It was during 1943, she was based near an American air base at Dunkeswell who were on operational flights over Germany. With the planes returning with their wounded, Wendy had the opportunity of saving life. In her spare time she visited the various military clubs and took part in the local activities. It was on such an occasion, when she attended a local dance, that she came in contact with the American air crews who were obviously always prepared to make the most of life. It was a case of 'here today and gone tomorrow'. Wendy's close friend was also a nurse who came from Norwich. Her name was Jill Taylor. She was another quiet person by nature, although before the war Jill had been a chorus girl and a trained speciality dancer. She had appeared in pantomime and music halls and she was very attractive with dark hair. Most of the stage folk were going overseas with ENSA, but Jill decided to play a more worthy and serious part in the war. So as great friends from different walks of life, both Wendy and Jill palled-up and when the opportunity came they would join the local festivities.

It was during one of these evenings that Wendy met a very handsome American by the name of Bob Wilder. He came from Kansas. His parents were farmers and he was very tall, and before the war he was in college studying law. His age was twenty-five and Wendy was now twenty-three. The chemistry between them was perfect he being rather shy and serious and having a very infectious smile. His hair was thick, black and curly. He had the Kansas drawl in his speech and he never seemed to know just what to do with his hands.

As the evening rolled on, Wendy felt this was her kind of fellow, but to think about falling in love just was not on with so much going on. The future looked grim, in fact she did not even get around to asking him if her was married, or had he a girlfriend waiting for him back in the States?

The time now was 11 p.m., and time to return to base. Both Wendy and Jill went back to their quarters, and Bob returned to his base. They were lucky in as much as there had not been an air raid.

Both girls exchanged comments about what had happened during the evening. Poor Jill had found herself with an undesirable wide boy from London, who was in the Army close by to the American air base, and getting rid of him was not easy easy.

As the next few weeks went by Bob's squadron was on operations over the Rhur and the losses were tremendous. So much so that the American Command decided to take only a few planes from different bases and rendezvous over a certain area before going onto the target. So although the losses were still very high, it was not so noticeable at each base because the whole task force no longer came from one base.

Whilst on these operations Bob saw very little of Wendy, but the spiv from London became a pest to Jill and tried to force his intentions on her. Wendy, who by now through her association with Bob and his squadron, mentioned this to a close friend of Bob's so it was only a matter of time before a couple of Yanks decided to discourage the soldier from the nearby barracks, whereby Jill was bothered no more.

It was now September 1944 and the friendship between Wendy and Bob had developed satisfactorily to the hopes that when the war was over they would take life more seriously and get married. She had by now found out a great deal about Bob through his fellow fliers and his commanding officer.

Bob was single, and his parents did own a farm. In fact it was a ranch, with a large head of cattle. The prospects between them both looked good — almost too good to last.

It was during September of 1944 that for the first time they had been able to arrange to have leave at the same time, so where else but in London to spend one week. So off they went as happy as could be. Bob had saved up his pocket money and so had Wendy. They booked in at the Grosvenor Hotel, close to Victoria Station. Their rooms were separate but next to each other. Wendy's room number was 101 and Bob's 102. After their arrival it was straight to the bar to celebrate with a drink. The whole atmosphere was one of love; Wendy looked radiant and Bob very handsome.

Leaving the bar they strolled arm in arm out into the street towards Victoria Street making their way towards the Houses of Parliament. Walking along the right-hand side of the street, they had to pass the Army and Navy Store; but alas Bob could not pass by, he just had to take Wendy inside, whereupon he made his way to the ladies' fashion counter. Wendy refused all his offers, but submitted to receiving a very delicate and charming scarf which she promptly arranged around her neck.

They then left the store and proceeded further along Victoria Street but could not resist Westminster Abbey and all of its history and its decor. As they approached the altar they both paused and Bob got hold of Wendy's hand and said "Will you marry me someday after the war?" His eyes had a charming gleam, his mouth had a smile.

Her reply was without hesitation, "Yes Bob, I want that more than anything else in the world."

Of all the conversations that they had before, this was the moment that words meant so much. They had embraced before with a gentle goodnight kiss, but the opportunity of closer commitment in the past was seldom experienced, but this moment was for real. Bob kissed her on the cheek and said "I love you, honey."

"I love you too" was Wendy's reply.

Once out of the abbey they strolled up Whitehall passing New Scotland Yard. Bob stopped and said "So this is the great Scotland Yard that I have heard so much about."

"Does it impress you, Bob?" asked Wendy.

"Oh yea" Bob said.

On their way they walked past Downing Street and on to Horse Guards Parade. Wendy just could not resist but to stand in front of a Household Cavalry rider and try to attract his attention by winking at him. But he did not move a muscle which amused Bob. "You know honey, I could not have resisted you if I had been him" said Bob.

So hand in hand they went on their way under Admiralty Arch towards Buckingham Palace and down The Mall. All this impressed Bob very much. They left the palace behind them and made their way to St. James's Palace and on to Piccadilly where they found Eros.

Arm in arm they strolled into Regent's Street where they came across a delightful jeweller's shop which Bob could not resist. They both looked into the window and did feast their eyes on a tray of rings. Bob looked at Wendy and said "Let me buy you a kind of engagement ring."

Wendy then said as she bit her lower lip "I don't know, Bob."

"Oh, come on, honey, it will be a link for us to start when the war is over." He had a serious look on his face.

Wendy wrinkled her nose and said "Why not?"

So into the shop they went.

They were greeted by a charming lady "Can I help you?" she said.

"Yep, I need to buy this young lady a ring for a keepsake." Bob said it was obvious that the romance had taken on a serious note and after much consultation a ring was chosen, and the shop's atmosphere was one of a very happy mood.

After the sale they made their way to the West End. Leicester Square was their next port of call for something to eat, and upon their arrival at a small restaurant in Charing Cross Road they were greeted with a smile from the proprietor. He found them a delightful secluded table for what appeared to him to be a lovesick couple.

This was Bob's first visit to the West End of London. A well-chosen wine was selected and Bob raised his glass and said "To us, honey." Wendy had never been happier. To think of all the tragedies that had happened to her, it looked as though her luck had changed.

The evening was spent in the Coliseum Theatre where 'Maid of the Mountain' was on with a cast of Sonny Hale, Malcolm Keen, Davy Burnaby and Elsie Randolph. When the show was over they grabbed a taxi back to their hotel just as the sirens started warning an air raid was about to begin. Back in the hotel bar they both agreed what a wonderful day it had been.

"If only the day would never end" is what Bob said, and Wendy looked at her ring — for it was the first time that she had ever worn a ring.

As Bob saw her to her room, he took her into his arms and caressed her with all the warmth within his heart and said "Thanks for a lovely day, honey."

She returned his kiss and complimented him by saying "You're the nicest man I have ever met. You're some hell of a gentleman Bob. I love you so much.''

I think those words said it all to what was a true love affair. But was it to last? The rest of the week was spent in complete harmony. Despite the air raids that continued on London their love survived. The final day arrived for them to leave London and their train journey was one of silence as they shared their love together.

## CHAPTER 13

In the weeks that followed, Wendy was very busy and her friend Jill took leave to go home to Norwich. Wendy saw her off at the station. It was a strange goodbye; first of all the train was late arriving which gave them both a lot of time in which to talk as they sat in the station cafe.

Suddenly their moments together ran out and Wendy said "Take care Jill, I will be waiting here for your return."

Jill stood motionless and with a slight smile upon her face she said "I'm glad we met and that you're so happy with Bob. Take care, Wendy." There was a pause in her voice then she said as they held each other tightly in their arms and kissed, "Goodbye Wendy."

As the train pulled out of the station with Jill hanging out of the window waving desperately goodbye, it struck Wendy that it might be the last time they would see each other. Little did she know then that her thoughts would come true, for Jill was killed at her parents' home during an air raid. Such news came to Wendy almost at the time Jill was to have returned. Wendy wondered if Jill had experienced a vision. Who knows?

Wendy's mind was taken off this tragedy because she was so busy attending to hospital affairs and life must go on. It was one night in the local pub that Bob said to her "When this war is over honey you must come to the States and meet my parents." His eyes looked tired as he and other fliers had been hard pushed on operations.

She took hold of his hand and said "Oh Bob, let's hope we come through this nightmare. I do so want to marry you."

The next day Bob was on a raid over Essen where Krupps Industries lay. Being daylight raids, the Americans were easy targets and easy prey for the German fighters. It was during this raid that Bob's plane was reported missing. Wendy made frantic enquiries as to what had happened, but the news was not good. Bob's plane had been seen crashing down in flames. It had been hit by ground gunfire. It was assumed that they were all killed or captured — they just did not know. Wendy felt that her life was now finished.

Time for Adolf Hitler was now running out. The Allied landings in Normandy were successful and as for Wendy she now lived in a small flat in Streatham. It was when she was walking home after her duties in the blackout that she unfortunately missed her footing and fell against a lamppost giving her head a nasty crack. After gaining control of herself she proceeded on her way, but she was still very much shaken up, and upon her arrival at her flat she took stock of the damage to her head. She was bleeding very badly on the forehead, and she did her best to bathe and dress the wound. It was during the night that she awoke with a terrible headache. As she got out of bed to make her way to the bathroom in order to get some headache tablets she discovered when putting on the light switch that she was still in darkness. She naturally assumed the bulb was faulty, but knowing where the tablets were she took two and returned to bed.

At 7 o'clock in the morning the alarm went off. She awoke, but to her surprise it was still dark. She tried not to panic but she came to the conclusion that she had concussion and could not see at all. She made her way to the flat next to hers and banged on the door.

The lady, Mrs Wise, opened her door only to see how distressed Wendy was. Without hesitation she assisted Wendy inside and sat her down, "What is it, my dear, what is the matter?" she asked.

"I cannot see — I am blind — please help me" Wendy said as tears started to trickle down her face.

"Sit still, my dear, I will call the doctor."

After what seemed ages to Wendy, Mrs Wise returned, "Now, my dear, don't worry, the doctor is coming." She made Wendy a cup of tea whilst Wendy explained what had happened on her way home.

The arrival of the doctor was most welcome. After his examination and listening to her experience, he arranged for her to go to hospital right away. Mrs Wise put a few things in a suitcase for Wendy, and travelled with her in the ambulance to see her admitted into the hospital.

During the following few days, Wendy underwent various tests, but unfortunately she had lost her sight. Poor Wendy lay in silence wondering just what was to become of her. Life had really been hard on this lovely girl, now almost twenty-five years old and it looked as though her life was now to be spent in total darkness. She had very few friends and the war was now almost over. Everybody was looking to a bright new future, but Wendy's was a dark one in more ways than one. With peacetime celebrations regarding the unconditional surrender of the German forces the world was about to move into a happier atmosphere and fear was about to disappear, but for dear Wendy fear for the first time in her life was to become her constant companion. It was obvious that short of a miracle she was to be blind for the rest of her life.

The hospital had done all it could. It was during the last few hours of her being in hospital that her luck changed as she made her way out to an awaiting hospital car clutching her small suitcase and with the help of one of the hospital staff the driver came to her assistance. She was soon being driven away. The driver was very silent and also very young but Wendy asked him his name.

"I'm Phillip Baker, and I live only a street away from where you live." His age was twenty-eight and he was single and he lived on his own. He was almost six feet tall and very reserved. It was next to no time before they arrived at Wendy's flat. He asked "Can I see you in?"

"That's kind of you" Wendy said, and so to her apartment they went. Once inside he could see what a hard life she was having, and being now blind it was going to be so much harder.

He got her settled in and said "If there is anything that I can do for you, please call me." He gave her his number and went through the motions with her for dialling his number.

He understood that a Mrs Wise would keep an eye on her but it was crystal clear to him that whatever arrangements had been made by the hospital to help her it was still going to be up-hill all the way.

Phillip made a point of popping in and out whenever he could; in fact he did the cooking. What Wendy did not know was what he looked like. All she knew was that he was a very pleasant fellow and demanded nothing from her.

As the weeks went by he treated her cautiously. By this time she was moving around her flat very well and in no time at all she was on a training course for having a dog — and very successful it was. Wendy began smiling again and Phillip was so happy doing what he could for her. It was much later that she found out that Phillip's mother was blind during the last years of her life, so it all made sense for him to know what to do for Wendy.

It was difficult to think that a romance would blossom out of their relationship, but it did. Wendy was so happy with Phillip and her dog called Micky, especially when Phillip suggested that they all went on a holiday to Devon for two weeks. It was in Devon that a miracle was performed.

They stayed in a delightful hotel called Ottery Farm Hotel where the floors were uneven and the plumbing left much to be desired, but at least they did accept dogs, and for the first week much fun was had. The food was very good and Micky could run around the grounds with ease, but during the second week something very odd happened. The owners of this hotel had many cats — seventeen in all — and this disturbed Micky somewhat, although the cats were kept very well under control. It was on the Monday morning of the second week when Wendy was going down the stairs to breakfast and holding onto the banisters tightly, that several cats rushed past her, and Micky who was following behind tried to protect her; unfortunately Micky being a large Alsatian accidentally pushed into Wendy throwing her down the stairs headfirst from top to bottom, and she remained motionless.

Micky stood by her side barking which brought Phillip to her rescue. He rushed down and gently picked her up "Take it easy darling, you are going to be alright. I will put you onto the lounge settee." Micky started to make a fuss of her by licking her face.

By this time the proprietor and his wife were at her side, "Shall we call a doctor?" asked the owner.

At that moment she opened her eyes then shut them. Her breathing had increased a little.

Phillip held her hand and said "How do you feel, darling?" She opened and shut her eyes many times. Phillip stared at her because he could see some change had taken place in her expression. Her eyes were now staring as she glanced from side to side. "What is it darling, you look strange?"

"I feel strange" Wendy said. She then looked at Phillip and said, "You're very handsome."

"You can see!" said Phillip.

"Yes, I can see" answered Wendy.

"The fall — that is what did it. We owe it all to Micky for pushing you downstairs."

They both grabbed Micky and kissed him. "What a wonderful dog you are" said Wendy. It truly was a miracle. The owners of the hotel just could not believe what they had witnessed. Wendy sat up and said "It is true I can see. It will stay like this won't it Phillip?"

"Of course it will. What happened long ago when you bumped your head this bump has reversed everything. It has done what medical science could not do" said Phillip.

By this time Wendy was now sitting up on the settee, when in came the owner's wife with a pot of tea and with a broad smile on her face, she said "Drink this, you deserve it, my dear, it has been wonderful to witness a miracle." She then left both of them to enjoy the tea and celebrate their good fortune.

Wendy was the first to speak "Oh Phillip, you have been so wonderful to me and now that your work and care for me is over you won't want me."

Phillip took one look at her and held her in his arms and said "I did what I did because I fell in love with you at the hospital. You're so lovely, and I did not propose to you because you may have thought it was in sympathy. Anyway now that you have seen me, perhaps you won't want me."

She put her arms around his neck and said "If you want me to be your wife, the answer is yes."

Phillip then said, "Wait until dinner tonight, I may have something to ask you that I have been waiting to do for a very long time."

At that moment they made their way to the breakfast room, and whilst sitting over breakfast, Phillip said, "Oh why wait for dinner tonight? Will you do me the honour and marry me, Wendy?"

She looked him straight in the eye then glanced down at Micky who was looking up towards her. She then turned and looked at Phillip and said, "Yes I do really love you, I am so happy. I have never been so lucky and my answer to you is yes, I want to marry you."

The second week of the holiday was a great success, but as the holiday came to a close after visiting Sidmouth, Branscombe, Beer, Exeter and many other wonderful places, their thoughts were on Micky because he would have to leave them and look after another blind person. They did wonder if they could keep him, but the only right thing to do was to let him go.

The weeks that followed were occupied with preparing for the wedding and arranging the return of Micky to take up other duties and to help another blind person. When the time came to part company it was a day of sadness indeed, but it had to be done. The other important thing was for Wendy now to find a job. She had no wish to return to nursing, but looked for a job that had more regular hours — so she found employment in a local building company where she was involved with the costing and the records concerning various contracts. What is more, the pay was good.

Soon the day arrived for them to get married. The banns were put up in the local church and most of the guests who were to attend the ceremony and reception were on Phillip's side, but the day was a great success and the honeymoon was for two weeks on the Italian mainland in Sorrento. They flew to Pisa and then by coach to Sorrento passing through Naples.

The Hotel Metropol was to be their home for two weeks, and what a delightful hotel it was! But to get to the beach, they had to walk across the road and down a pathway to the rocky beach. The sand of course was black, due to Mount Vesuvius erupting two thousand years ago, but for all that the sea was calm, warm and blue and it was very clean for swimming.

Wendy could not believe her luck to be able to see and visit places such as Amalfi, Positano, Pompeii and of course the wonderful and majestic island of Capri. How romantic it all was, and on their return home the coach stopped for them to visit the Leaning Tower of Pisa. The evenings they spent dancing to Italian love songs would be remembered for the rest of their lives.

They returned to England very happy and very brown, but one other great thing had to take place; the love they made together was the beginning of a beautiful daughter. It was six weeks after their returning to England that Wendy showed signs of motherhood. The year was then 1947.

During the following nine months, before baby arrived, Phillip was busy with his taxi service and Wendy with her job in the building company. The name to be given to the new arrival was to be if a boy, Phillip, if a girl, Phyllis. Life is very strange waiting for the unexpected, but Wendy had a very disturbing dream and screamed out in horror. Phillip grabbed hold of her and comforted her by holding her tightly. She was perspiring but this dream was for real, and one that she could not tell Phillip.

As he calmed her down, she said "I'm alright now dear, it was just a nightmare."

"I guess it's because of your concern of having a baby?" Phillip said.

In the morning the day started as normal with Phillip off on his taxi trips and Wendy to her office. The dream began to haunt her as she sat on the bus travelling to work. She looked out of the window.

A fellow passenger spoke to her and said "It's a lovely day I hope it stays like this as my husband and I are going to America next week to visit relatives in Philadelphia."

"That's nice," said Wendy. "Have you ever been to the United States?"

Wendy paused as her mind drifted back to Bob Wilder the American airman whom she met during the war.

By the time she was about to answer, the lady said "Excuse me but I must get off here."

Still in deep thought of the past Wendy said, "Oh I am sorry, have a good trip to Uncle Sam next week." The odd thing was that it broke her dream which was about Bob Wilder. For no reason at all she saw the Flying Fortress that he was flying in was in a mass of flames, but Bob was falling out of the bomber and coming towards her with his face all disfigured and covered in blood. Suddenly she realised that she had to get off of the bus. During her short walk to the office she just could not get Bob out of her mind. It was obvious to her that Bob had been killed in that raid.

Putting all this now behind her she carried out her usual duties in the office. For days the dream haunted her and as the weeks rolled by, Phillip showed great concern about her, but somehow she always managed to give him the impression that all was well. She had one month to go before baby arrived. Would it be a boy or a girl? Great excitement was now being experienced and Wendy now had to stop work.

This particular day seemed no more unusual than any other day except what Phillip said — "Well darling, I'm off once again, be good and look after our little girl." With a big kiss and a hug he disappeared out of the front door and drove off in his taxi with a wave as he went.

Dear Wendy was left with just her thoughts, the day seemed to go by no differently to any other day except that the door bell rang around 5 o'clock which Wendy thought was a friend. Alas, as she opened the door there stood a policeman and a policewoman.

"Mrs Baker?" the policeman said.

"Yes" said Wendy.

"May we come in, Madam?"

As they both walked into the lounge, Wendy said "It's my husband. What has happened?"

"Please sit down" said the policewoman as she held Wendy's hand. "We have sad news, my dear" the policewoman said.

Wendy bit her bottom lip and said "Oh no!"

As tears started to find their way down her cheeks the policeman then said, "The fact of the matter is, Mrs Baker, your husband was involved in a multi-pile-up on the A23. Four vehicles were involved one of which was a large removal van." He paused, then said "He was on his own travelling back from a fare from Gatwick when he was pushed towards the centre barrier. He died instantly." He carried on by saying, "Two other people were killed and others injured."

The room was silent for the next few minutes then Wendy said "Where is he now?"

The policewoman took hold of Wendy's hand and said "In the local hospital."

"I would like to go now to see him please."

As she collected her things, also her thoughts, she could not help but think of Phil's last words as she sat in the police car 'Well darling, I'm off once again. Be good and look after our girl.'

Upon arrival at the hospital, great care and attention was given to Wendy by the police officers. As she slowly walked through the avenue of corridors, she wondered what awaited her at the end. Suddenly they stopped. They were met by a doctor and a sister.

A door was opened, and the doctor said "Now Mrs Baker, be strong." He and the sister held her arm firmly as she gazed down upon Phil. He had been cleaned up but his dear face was badly injured.

Wendy took a long look at him and said, "I now understand, Phil, God be with you, my darling. I'm sure it will be a girl."

As they all walked out of the room the two police officers closed in, but Wendy's legs gave way as they held her, and they slowly sat her in a seat. A cup of tea was provided, for her silence seemed to be the main comfort as a sedative was given to Wendy by the sister. An hour had now passed and it was decided that Wendy should return home. The policewoman suggested that she stayed a while and this is what happened until a neighbour came in to take over. Wendy thanked the police officers for their kindness, it is something she will always remember and be grateful that such a service exists.

# CHAPTER 14

As the days and weeks went by, Wendy realised that the terrible nightmare she had was not of Bob but of Phil, and as the days passed by and the evenings dragged on she was left with only her memories — some happy and some not so happy. Phil's relatives saw more of Wendy as the time got closer for the baby to arrive. Was it to be a girl or a boy? Wendy was now very strong, and had come to terms with the fact that she was to be alone with only her future child. With so much unhappiness in the past, surely having a baby was to be the turning point in her life.

With a watchful eye by a nearby neighbour Wendy's condition was fast approaching the birth of the little one. And so it was around 9 a.m. one sunny morning Wendy was taken to the local hospital where in the early hours of the following day, a bonny baby girl was born. The name chosen for such a charmer was to be Phyllis who weighed 7½lbs and looked very content in her mother's arms.

On their arrival home neighbours and Phil's relatives gathered around and made a great fuss of both of them, and after a short time arrangements were made to assist Wendy in order that she could return to work on a part-time basis. It was obvious to see that Wendy would never marry again. Both mother and daughter settled down to a way of life. All of Wendy's spare time was spent with Phyllis as she watched the little one grow up to a charming and beautiful young lady.

The year is now 1967 and Phyllis is now twenty and her

mother forty-seven and still not a grey hair on her head, in fact Wendy has become more attractive as she has got older. Several men have pursued her, some married and some single, but she has kept them all at bay. I wonder why? I ask myself perhaps there is something special yet to come, for those past twenty years have been very happy and many holidays have been spent together, and not once has Phyllis caused her mother to worry over anything. Both mother and daughter were inseparable until they went to the Greek Island of Corfu.

This was their first visit to Greece, so with their cases packed and a taxi waiting they were soon on their way to Gatwick. Phyllis was radiant and her mother was also looking beautiful. Gatwick had all the excitement and glamour in those days.

It was Wendy who broke silence and said, "You know, Phyllis, I am so happy when I am with you."

"So am I, Mother, when I am with you."

The hustle and bustle of the airport makes everything so great. They made their way to the coffee lounge and also bought a paper or two just to pass the time on the journey, with so many happy people and the attentive staff coming and going and the constant voice over the microphone announcing various situations applicable to the modern day of travel. Suddenly a call came for them to board their flight, and so they were soon airborne and on their way to the magical Island of Corfu in the sun. Food was provided and almost three hours later they were approaching the runway which first of all starts with the sea either side, which makes one cock an eyebrow to the approach. But in no time at all it was 'touch down' on the tarmac.

The first thing that Phyllis said when leaving the plane was "Phew, it's hot. It's like walking into a furnace."

The airport itself is not that large and so when collecting your baggage the conditions are rather cramped. You are quickly moved through customs and onto your awaiting coach. Both mother and daughter were so happy that only good could come out of this holiday. The coach, now full, pulled away from the airport and made its journey southwards along the coast of the Ionian Sea towards a delightful village called Messonghi, where their hotel, Messonghi Beach, awaited them.

The hotel was rather large. It accommodated about 1,500 people and it had its own beach. Its position on the island was on the east side and south of Corfu town which was approximately fifteen miles away, and was the last hotel on that side going south. The evening entertainment in store for them was a number of local tavernas in the nearby village called Moraitica.

Having now unpacked they both took a breather and gazed out of their window across the Ionian Sea where the Greek mainland could be observed. The first thing Phyllis said to her mother was "It's lovely, Mum. If only we could live here."

Her mother smiled and grabbed Phyllis by the arm and said "Yes it's really beautiful and I'm looking forward to my holiday."

After a wash and brush up they were soon down the stairs and out in front of the hotel which had a magnificent forecourt and drive to the main road. They strolled away from the hotel and took a small road when in next to no time they came across a delightful taverna called Christo's Bar.

Wendy said "Shall we try their tea here?"

Phyllis agreed. Once inside, a charming Greek waiter came to their assistance. They soon found out that they held Greek dances during the evenings and were persuaded to return that evening.

The hotel dinner was extremely good and so on a full stomach they walked out into the warm summer air towards the taverna. To their surprise they could hear Greek music being played which was coming from several tavernas so they had a choice. Nevertheless they made up their minds to go to Christo's Bar which on arrival was rather busy. There were of course holiday people and quite a lot of local Greeks.

The dancing was in full swing. The Greek waiter who had met them previously came to their table instantly and with the bouzouki music playing such tunes as 'O'Tapzan-O'Tapzan' and 'Syrtaki My Love'. The atmosphere was one of great happiness. In no time at all Phyllis was encouraged to join in to learn Greek dancing. Even Wendy was taken from the table and joined the dancing circle. Round and round in harmony with the music — tourists and locals enjoyed themselves. The evening rolled on until, to Wendy and Phyllis's surprise, the time was 1 a.m., and it was time for them to return to the hotel.

Whilst walking along the narrow road Phyllis said "It's lovely here, Mum."

"Yes, darling, I am enjoying myself very much."

The walk down the long drive to the hotel was lined with various flags of many countries. Once inside at the reception Wendy asked "May we have our key for room number 333?"

"Certainly, Madam. If there is anything you require please ring room service." Wendy smiled and thanked him.

Once in their room they were quick to put their heads on the pillow and into a deep sleep they both went.

In no time at all the morning sun had arrived. Phyllis was first out of bed and the view that greeted her was beyond her wildest dreams, for being on the third floor she had a panoramic view across the well-laid-out lawns and flowerbeds with dozens of bush roses which made their way to the private sandy beach, kissed by the Ionian Sea, which made its way far across to the Greek mainland. The view looking to the north one could see the Albanian coastline. To Phyllis it was breathtaking and so peaceful. The hotel stood in its own vast land with no other hotel or buildings nearby.

Wendy joined her daughter and said "Come on let's get washed and go down to breakfast."

What lay ahead of them in the next two weeks was to be unforgettable and was to remain with them forever.

The breakfast room was full of tourists all occupying their own individual tables. The movement of the attending staff was one of action, the breakfast was of continental style. After breakfast both Wendy and Phyllis stripped for action in their swim gear.

Down the stairs and out across the lawns through pathways lined with roses and onto the sandy beach where others were lazily laying around to absorb the Grecian sun. So they both grabbed a deck chair and started their Greek tan. The time was passed by turning from one direction to the other.

Soon Wendy suggested "Why don't we hire a car and travel the island?"

"What a good idea" said Phyllis.

Within moments they were back at the reception desk making a call to Costas Car Hire whose office was in Corfu town.

After lunch time a car arrived and details were exchanged. The driver who brought the car along was a very charming Greek called Spyros which of course is a very popular name on Corfu. More than half the men are called Spyros because that was the name of the patron saint, and it is in St. Spyridon Church that the saint's relics are kept. The church itself inside is very ornate and outside it is impressive with its tall tower containing the bells and a beautiful clock. The top of the tower has a pink dome and it is this church that Wendy and Phyllis visited during their first car ride from the Messonghi Beach Hotel. The drive took them through the small village of Moraitika where once a Roman villa stood and the remains can still be found. Further on they passed Benitses which is a small fishing village. It is at this point that the Kaiser Wilheim II of Germany used to anchor his private yacht the SS *Deutschland*. He would then travel through a village called Perama to the Achillion Palace in Gastoúri which he bought from the family of Elizabeth Empress of Austria after her being assassinated in Switzerland and who built the palace in 1890.

After this very scenic drive along the coast, Wendy pulled her car into the main car park in Corfu town where cricket is still played on the green, which faces the Volta at the Liston. These famous arcades are identical to those in Paris known as Rue de Rivoli which was built by the French during the French occupation of Corfu.

The town took both Wendy and Phyllis by storm because of its Venetian buildings built during the Venetian occupation and of its side roads with many Grecian shops and cafes. The whole of their afternoon was spent amongst the true Greeks, pushing their wheelbarrows and driving their three-wheel carts around the narrow streets. Phyllis could not take her eyes off looking into the sky where between the buildings hung washing out to dry. Finally their visit finished by sitting under the arcades sipping a cool drink with ice and indulging in eating the magnificent cakes that can be found. As the tourists and Greeks passed their table, smiles and words of joy were exchanged. The chatter of the Greeks, the occasional dog trotting along made the time a wonderful way to relax.

Wendy said "To think we have two whole weeks of this, I cannot believe it."

In no time at all they were soon on their way back along the coast road to their hotel. The parking of their car was no problem and the view from their bedroom was one of joy. It gave a panoramic view of the Ionian Sea with the Greek mainland clearly seen in the distance.

After freshening up and dressing appropriately for dinner, they made their way down to the dining room. Once seated at their individual table and making their choice, from the menu given by the waiter, they then sat and looked around the vast restaurant. Wendy could not contain herself, she had to say "I'm so happy, darling, this really is a wonderful island."

Phyllis gave a sigh and with her lips pulled tightly and her eyes gleaming with happiness she answered "Where in the world is there charm and peace like this Mummy?"

The waiter returned with their starter — melon, only to be followed by red mullet, a beautiful fish with all the vegetables that one could eat, with a well-chosen Greek wine called Porto Carras which is a white dry wine. The dessert was a well-chosen fruit dish with a large quantity of ice cream. To make pigs of themselves they enjoyed coffee and a small brandy called Mataxus.

It was after dinner that it all happened. Phyllis said "What shall we do?"

"Well darling, how about a stroll into that nearby village where music is coming from?" said Wendy.

So arm in arm like two sisters, they set off to the taverna called Anna's Bar. It could be clearly seen. The air was warm, and the sky was clear. The approach was along a rugged lane amongst olive trees which is the main industry of the island. They predominate the island and there are thought to be around 3,000,000 olive trees on Corfu. Talking of figures, it is well to know that the Greek population on Corfu is about 100,000 at the most.

The taverna that they visited was an old type which local Greeks visit a great deal. Once inside they were soon involved in the traditional dancing. Both Wendy and Phyllis were of course all arms and legs, but at least a great deal of fun was to be had. It was during this evening that a very handsome young man, also on holiday, from England on his own spotted Phyllis dancing. Suddenly she became aware that this fellow was taking a great deal of notice of her. After the dance they all returned to their tables.

The evening was a great success, and for Wendy and Phyllis it ended around 11 p.m. when they returned to their hotel. No comment was made regarding the young man.

The next day started with its usual hot sun and blue sky.

"Well Mum, where shall we go today?" asked Phyllis with deep thought and a smile on her face.

Wendy said "How about motoring to the north of the island?"

So with map well placed on the car bonnet it was decided to make their way to Kassíopi which lies on the east side. It was during their journey, after passing through Corfu town on the coast road, that they decided to pull into a delightful wide bay with long sandy beaches called Barbati. They found on the beach a taverna and a warm welcome to a cup of coffee. To their surprise sitting at a table all on his own was the young man they had seen the previous evening at Anna's Bar. He glanced in their direction. As they sat at a table a waiter was soon to attend to them.

"That's the fellow we saw last night, Mum" Phyllis said, and also showing a little interest.

"That's right" answered Wendy.

Coffee was now placed on their plastic tablecloth. They both sat in silence. Their eyes moved back and forth to each other.

Wendy broke the silence by saying "We can hardly talk to him, dear."

"You're right" said Phyllis.

Then to their surprise the fellow rose from his table and

walked towards the counter to pay his bill, after which he strolled away from the taverna and grabbed a bike that was leaning against a wall before riding off. He turned and glanced at Phyllis, then with a smile on his face he raised his eyebrows, pouted his lips, shrugged his shoulders, gave a cheeky wink and cycled away.

"Oh well" said Wendy.

"What does that mean?" Phyllis said.

"It means I think he is alone and you are not, and what can he do about it" said Wendy.

So they also were on their way to Kassíopi which is a small town tucked away in the corner of the island. It was at this place that a Roman town existed by the name of Cassiope which was visited by the Emperor Nero. After much exploring and the occasional swim, a return journey was made to Moraitika, the village close to their hotel. It was without doubt a very successful day.

After dinner that evening they made their way to Anna's Bar again, but Phyllis was disappointed when to her surprise the fellow did not turn up. In fact they did not see him again during the remaining period of their holiday.

As the rest of the holiday took shape great happiness was enjoyed by both mother and daughter. It was indeed a wonderful holiday and the thought of the young man had drifted out of Phyllis's mind.

The day arrived when they had to say goodbye to Corfu; a sad day indeed. The coach arrived outside the hotel and all the holiday-makers clambered on board as it journeyed along the eastern coast road. Quietness echoed as the passengers remained silent. Soon the coach pulled off the road and into the airport car park where all the passengers and baggage was withdrawn from the coach and everybody made their way to the check-in point. It was whilst this painful procedure was taking place and Wendy and Phyllis were buying the odd paper and magazine, that the young man appeared on the scene. He stood close to Phyllis. When she turned her head their eyes came in contact with each other and within seconds both said "Hello".

Then a smile became a predominant feature as the fellow

said "We meet again. Have you had a good holiday?"

"Oh yes" said Phyllis just as Wendy came alongside. "Oh" said Phyllis, "this is my mother."

The fellow stared at Wendy and stretched out his hand, "Pleased to meet you. My name is John Pike."

Phyllis was quick to say, "Mine is Phyllis."

There are two things you can do at Corfu airport: you can use the cafe facilities before checking-in, or John was quick to suggest that they have a cup of tea or coffee with him after checking-in. The airport was very busy as it's not too large to cope with the volume of people coming and going and it is also very noisy. However, with all three now seated, John was soon to join them over a cup of coffee. It was clear to see that Phyllis liked his company. He was tall with thick fair hair. His manner was one of a quiet nature and rather shy. His hands showed signs of hard work and his age being around twenty-five. The conversation was centred around him as he explained that he was single and lived at home with his mother and father. He also explained that he was a motor mechanic and was employed by a large repair company situated in Croydon not far from where he lived. Regarding his holiday, it was his first package holiday abroad.

By this time the preliminary explanations were over and it was being announced that their flight was now boarding at gate number 3. He was, of course, very attentive right up until they boarded the plane. The day was of course very hot as they walked towards the plane. Unfortunately when they were all on the plane they were separated — John's seat was at the rear of the plane whilst Wendy and Phyllis sat up front. It was obvious that Phyllis was thinking about John and he was doing likewise. Upon arrival at Gatwick, and during their collecting their baggage, John did not lose sight of them, so once through customs he made his way to them and said, "It's been nice meeting you both. Would it be possible to keep in touch?"

Both Wendy and Phyllis answered simultaneously "That would be nice."

Then they all laughed. So telephones and addresses were exchanged with a farewell goodbye.

## CHAPTER 15

During the first week back at work, poor Phyllis found herself thinking about John and she could not resist but to mention about him to her workmates, so it was obvious that she had fallen in love. It was one evening around 8 o'clock that the phone ran and she rushed to pick it up.

"Hello," said Phyllis.

"Hello," said John. "Did you arrive home safely?"

Phyllis was so pleased to hear from him that she tried to be calm and said "Yes, thank you. Did you?"

He then went on by saying "Would it be possible for you to have a meal one evening with me?"

Her answer was of course "I would love to."

After their long chat of pleasurable conversation, a romance had just been born. Both were happy and both were looking forward to their meeting the following Saturday when they would dine alone in a local restaurant at 8 p.m. John would pick her up at 7 p.m.

The love affair between them got off to a good start. During their first date the romance blossomed and Wendy knew that some day they would marry. It was that obvious, which meant that a certain amount of loneliness lay ahead for her.

Almost two years has now passed and wedding bells were inevitable. July was the month set for the big occasion. The big disappointment was, of course, that her father would not be giving her away.

The day arrived for the wedding. Phyllis looked beautiful,

all in white, and John a very handsome groom. It was a dear friend of John's who gave Phyllis away, and another friend of John's who was best man. The reception was held at the Selsdon Park Hotel after which many photographs were taken in the magnificent gardens of the hotel. Their honeymoon was planned for Rome — a city of love — with so much to see; and of course the Island of Capri had to be one of many places to be visited. As for Wendy, her life was about to take on a different aspect.

Upon their return from their honeymoon, they started their marriage in a small flat above a shop, and as time rolled on they became restless for something different in life. It became very clear to Wendy that they wanted to leave England and start a new life. But where?

During the following weeks, with a great deal of thinking they made up their minds to try America. John made the necessary enquiries and applied for several jobs that were going at the time in Philadelphia for motor mechanics. He eventually had success, and so after going through the medical requirements both he and Phyllis applied for a visa, and finally they were accepted into America.

Wendy's heart sank as she felt that her own little world was about to crumble. She realized that it was their lives that were now important, and America offered them so much. It was of course, Phyllis and John's wish that Wendy would join them also, as there would be nothing in England for her.

Alas the time had come for them to depart for America, and so at Heathrow Airport all three had sad faces. It was Phyllis who said to her mother, "Please, Mum, try and come to see us soon."

Wendy looked at both of them and said, "Just as soon as you get settled I will come, I promise. Who knows I may wish to join you forever."

At that moment their aircraft was ready for boarding, so with the last hugs and kisses and the shedding of tears the couple made their way through the departure barrier. Within moments they had gone out of sight, leaving Wendy to wait and see their plane take off on its way to the United States. She then returned to her house that was empty once again.

Wendy's day often started by opening her mail first thing

in the morning, and this particular day she received a letter from a solicitor whose client was an old lady who had recently died. He informed Wendy that a certain Mrs Mathews had mentioned Wendy in her will, and he was asking Wendy to contact him in order to make the necessary arrangements for her to visit his office as soon as possible.

The lady's name meant something to her, because she had attended her when she was a patient in Wendy's hospital during the war. But Wendy was kind to everybody, so why should she be special to this lady puzzled Wendy. However she contacted the solicitor that very day and an appointment was made for that week.

On the day of the appointment Wendy made her way to the solicitor's office. He was an elderly gentleman who asked her to be seated. He then proceeded to read out the part of the will that concerned Wendy. Apparently, Mrs Mathews had a piece of 17th century property in Layhembury in East Devon, which she used over the years as a holiday home. Of course, it was not used during the war so it had been very much neglected. Nevertheless, because of the kindness and attention given to her by Wendy she had made the property over to her upon her death.

The solicitor said, "I found it very difficult to trace you. That is why it has been so long notifying you of this request. However, I managed it by starting at the hospital where you worked during the war." Wendy looked very puzzled and found it very difficult to take it all in. The solicitor then said, "I have the freehold deeds of the property which Mrs Mathews has owned for thirty-five years, and which I am instructed to hand over to you.

The formality of the paperwork was the easy part. The difficult part was for Wendy to realise her good fortune from a perfect stranger. Obviously, the old lady took a shine to her and thought that the property would do Wendy much more good than anything else. With the interview now over and the keys firmly held in her hand, she had only to visit the property in her own good time.

When she arrived home she not only made herself a nice pot of tea, she was also quick to open a map of East Devon and located Layhembury which was between Ottery St. Mary and Sidmouth. She decided to drive to Devon the following weekend. The weather was good, and so with a few things packed she made an early start. With her thoughts of Phyllis in America, and thinking perhaps of joining her one day she gave a great deal of thought to the fact that if she sold the property it would give her an income to retire on.

The traffic on the roads was not busy, and half way on the journey she stopped to relax over a cup of coffee. She then continued until she saw a sign to Ottery St. Mary, and it was here she decided to have a spot of lunch. She found a car park in the town and she was able to explore the town with ease. She found this town to be rather small but charming. In the High Street could be found the usual local shops and of course a very delightful restaurant where she was able to have a reasonable meal. The tables and chairs were of Austrian style and the proprietors were so charming. She enjoyed her lunch and was able to check where Layhembury was.

After lunch she strolled around the town and found many shops of interest, she was very taken with Ottery St. Mary but she had to tear herself away in order to find the cottage which was about four miles from Sidmouth. She turned off the main road at Newton Cross and down a narrow road where she passed several thatched cottages. All of a sudden there was the cottage called 'The Willows'. She drove into the drive with ease and stopped. As she got out of the car the silence that surrounded the property was very noticeable. Naturally, the garden and cottage had been badly neglected. As she approached the front door it all seemed very inviting. The door creaked as she opened it. The flooring was a little uneven which was only to be expected — after all, the building was 17th century. From the hall she walked into the lounge where an old log fire stood. The beams in the ceiling were low and made it very dark. She then strolled back into the hall and then into the dining room. She noticed the old carpets on the bare boards, and so made her way to the kitchen which had an electric cooker — all in good condition. There were plenty of cupboards and a modern sink; there was also a utility room with a fridge and washing-machine. As she made her way upstairs the walls seemed to close in on her and the stairs were very uneven. The cottage had four bedrooms and a bathroom-cum-toilet. It had been reasonably looked after but much needed to be done to bring it up to her way of life. Nevertheless it was a gift and it all seemed very inviting.

Wendy decided to stay a few days and so she made her way out of the cottage and drove to a nearby inn to book a reservation. She thought the beds needed airing so she booked into the 'Ploughman's Inn'. It was a warm and cosy pub and the locals were of a very friendly nature.

It was at the bar that evening, before her meal, that she introduced herself as the new owner of 'The Willows'. The conversation was met with a stony silence. The innkeeper turned to serve another customer just as an elderly gentleman said to Wendy, "I hope you will be happy there. Will it be your permanent address?"

Wendy looked at him and said, "Well, I inherited it from a Mrs Mathews who died recently, but I shall use it as a holiday home if I keep it."

The gentleman then said, "I think that's a good idea."

Wendy got the impression that there was more than meets the eye with the cottage. However, she was served with her drink and enjoyed her meal.

Her first night at the inn was an enjoyable one, and the next day she returned to the cottage for a further look around. Also, she spent much time in the garden, which had potential regarding making it attractive. She made up her mind that she would return in a week or two and spend a short holiday there just to get to know the place and the surrounding countryside.

As the weeks went by, Wendy got the urge to return to Layhembury. It was as though something was pulling her back, so she made preparations to motor down to Devon. The journey was very pleasant and she arrived late evening and intended to stay there for two weeks. She had taken fresh bed linen to make herself comfortable, and after a nightcap she retired to bed. The next couple of days were spent around the area. It was all very quiet — even the nearby church seemed to have very little activity. In fact, when she visited the church she found it all very dark, and there was not a resident vicar only one who came every now and then. He had several parishes that he took in turn to visit and hold services.

After just three days in the cottage, she went to her wardrobe to wear another pair of leather shoes and when she looked at them they were covered with mildew caused through some form of dampness. She had never experienced this before and thought it was because the cottage was so old and damp. She soon became aware that the place smelt damp and when she decided at the end of the first week to vacuum the place, she looked under the furniture and saw how damp they really were. She realized that this was no place for her to own. However, she was enjoying her stay until one night during the second week of her stay she was woken up due to a strange noise which appeared to be outside. As she sat up in bed she saw the bedroom door open very slowly and there stood a lady with a young six-year-old girl. They both looked at Wendy but said nothing. Then they disappeared. It took Wendy by surprise. She sat motionless for some time then she realised that they were dressed in clothing of the 17th century and their faces were white. A cold shiver ran down Wendy's spine for she then realised that they were ghosts. There was no mistaking what she had seen, yet she was not afraid — but it was unpleasant. Nothing further happened that night.

The following day she spent in Ottery St. Mary doing a spot of shopping. In the evening she attended a local get-together where folk display their cooking exhibits for prizes to be won — also various plants and needlework. It was during this evening that she learned a great deal about the village. It was, of course, a very poor village and had always been this way. She also found out that Oliver Cromwell and his men had stayed in the village and had occupied several cottages. Plunder and rape had of course taken place, which made her wonder if something terrible had happened in her cottage. It played on her mind. However, the evening was a pleasant one with the locals. There was a very kind elderly couple who were born in the village and had been farmers all their life, but were now retired. They introduced themselves as Bert and Rosie. It was Rosie who made her way to Wendy.

She looked Wendy up and down then said, "How are you, my dear?"

"I am fine," answered Wendy. She then continued by

saying, "The village folk are very nice and very active by the look of their exhibits."

"Well, my dear, their lives are very narrow," was Rosie's reply.

Then Bert said, "Do you like the cottage, and is everything alright?" He had an odd look on his face which puzzled Wendy as though he was expecting her to say something mysterious.

"Everything is just fine," said Wendy.

"Will you use it as a holiday home, my dear?" asked Rosie.

"I'm not sure. I may have other plans."

Both Bert and Rosie needed to know more about Wendy and this is why they tried chatting her up.

"You will excuse me," Wendy said, "but I would like to speak with the vicar."

"Yes, of course," said Rosie.

The vicar was a young man, maybe in his late forties. He was chatting to a few locals, one of which looked like a retired army colonel who turned and stared at Wendy. He said, "Tell me, my dear, is everything alright at 'The Willows'?"

"You know, you are the second person to ask me if everything is alright at 'The Willows'."

"Well, my dear, let me introduce myself. I am Colonel Jenkins and it's just that we locals want newcomers to be happy and content, that is all."

Wendy took her time, then said, "It's very kind of you all to be so concerned." She then turned to the vicar with a smile and said, "I understand you have several parishes under your control?"

He was a charming person and said, "You are right, I am kept very busy, but should you need me, please call me, I am only a phone call away."

She had a long conversation with him and she became aware that he was concerned about her — especially when he made one remark: "You are there alone?"

"Yes" said Wendy.

"Then, like I said, if I can be of any assistance at any time do not hesitate to telephone me."

"I will remember that" said Wendy.

At this point she turned away and lost herself amongst the people. Soon she made her way out of the hall and into the quiet, peaceful night with a full moon looking down upon her.

As she left the hall behind her, she strolled along a stony lane which led her over a fast-running stream where apparently someone had drowned mysteriously not long ago. The noise and the roar of the stream got louder as she hurried away into silence. She then passed a very old large thatched cottage known as 'The Lower Heath' where Oliver Cromwell actually stayed when he visited his troops. She experienced a cold feeling as she passed by, and after passing a few very old thatched cottages she passed a small village post office and a garage and the village school. Finally she reached the entrance of her cottage. It looked very peaceful. In fact, too good to be true for she had always been used to noise such as town traffic and people around her. Layhembury itself was a very quiet place and to go anywhere you had to drive several miles along narrow roads with high hedges. It was dangerous should you venture to walk such roads, and so it was obvious to Wendy that since she had not been born in such surroundings with farmland of cattle and sheep and of her being alone it really was not for her. And since it seemed that the place was haunted she had no other choice but to return home to Surrey and make plans to perhaps join her daughter in the United States.

She stayed just one more night in 'The Willows'. It was this night that convinced her that something was trying to get her to stay or to drive her away. The evening was rather chilly and so she thought she would light the log fire for a little extra warmth. It was whilst she was sitting quietly reading an old local paper she became aware that the log fire almost went out and then it would blaze away as though it was controlled by someone. She ignored it and went on to read that many years ago a young couple that were driving through Layhembury stopped to ask the way to Exeter at the local garage; they were never seen again, only the car was found abandoned.

Wendy then decided to call it a day and retire to bed. With

the fire now safely out, she made her way up the uneven, stairway. As she entered the bedroom she noticed that the wardrobe door was just closing. She paused for a moment then she made her way towards it with caution then opened the door and looked inside. To her amazement there was nothing there. She put it all down to a draught. The room was nicely furnished and had very heavy velvet curtains. She sat on the bed for a little while letting her mind wander over the past years, then finally got into bed and turned off the bedside lamp. Within moments, before dropping off into a deep sleep she was aware that she was not alone. Above the ceiling of her bedroom, over by the door, heavy feet walked slowly from one corner of the bedroom to the other passing right over her bed. Then it stopped for a moment. It then turned and proceeded to walk back towards the door. Now, Wendy knew that no one could walk normally in the loft because of the rafters and these old cottages did not have a boarded loft. As she sat up in bed it walked again in the same direction and then stopped again. She did not panic, but calmly put on the bedside lamp. She then got out of bed and went and undid the door to look out onto the landing but of course there was no one there. She was convinced that whatever it was, it was in the loft. However, she went back to bed and lay quietly for several minutes but heard no more. She was sure that what she had heard was boots worn by a man. She finally fell asleep.

In the morning she went into Ottery St. Mary and visited an estate agent with the object of putting the property on the market. A value for the cottage was agreed. She also informed him that she may sell her property in Surrey and leave England to settle in the United States. After exchanging various details such as her solicitor, she then said that she would be pleased to hear from him after he had visited the cottage and put a selling price on it. She then left him the keys and was on her way out of Devon and on to Surrey.

As the following weeks passed by, Wendy slowly came to terms that she would go to America, and so she waited to hear from Phyllis. It was not too long before she received a letter telling her that they had found a house and that John was really settling down to his job and proving a success at it. She was also given to understand that a very kind gentleman at the estate office had been a great help regarding their getting such a lovely house — they spoke very highly of him. The other news was that Phyllis was expecting a baby in about six months, so this made Wendy very very excited.

As the months passed Wendy knitted a few things for the new baby and soon it was known to be a girl that had arrived. But what was to be her name?

So the odd phone call was made until Wendy said, "Well, Phyllis, if you are stuck why don't you call her Jill after my very dear friend Jill Taylor whom I met in the last war?"

Much to Wendy's surprise Phyllis said "That's not a bad idea, I will call her Jill and Wendy."

And so it was agreed.

It was after the birth of Jill that Wendy agreed to go to America for the christening and stay for a few weeks. So Wendy made her way to the travel agents to arrange her flight ticket. Being now full of excitement she looked a young girl once again.

As she walked into the travel office she was greeted by a very young and attractive female assistant, "Can I help you?"

"I hope so," said Wendy.

"Please sit down," said the young girl. After making herself comfortable the young lady said, "Where do you wish to go?"

With a long pause and a smile on her face Wendy said "The United States. I wish to visit my daughter."

At that point in time the young lady frowned a little as she looked at Wendy and said, "Are you American?"

"Oh no, my daughter and her husband live there because of his job."

"When do you wish to travel and to what part of the USA?"

Wendy was quick to answer, "My daughter lives in Philadelphia, but I think I would like to fly to New York and stay a day in order to see the city. Then my family would meet me there and drive me to their home."

"Well, we have a flight to New York next Monday if this will do?" said the young lady with a gleam in her eye.

L

Wendy said, "That will do nicely."

With the details arranged and the payment made Wendy was all set for a new phase in her life. As she walked out of the travel agent's office she felt relieved, as though the future was planned. Soon she made her way to various shops where she purchased the odd gift to take with her for the family. Wendy's life had not been a bowl of cherries but perhaps the gods were about to change all that — for that is exactly what happened.

She arrived back at her house and promptly made a cup of tea then without further delay she made the necessary phone call to Phyllis.

John answered, "Hello Mum, how are you?"

Her answer was quick, "John, I have made flight arrangements to fly to New York next Monday and I will check into an hotel so that I can look around the city. Perhaps you could pick me up the following day and take me to your home? Is Phyllis there?"

"Hang on."

Great excitement could be heard as Phyllis grabbed the phone, "Hello Mum, it's great news. We will be picking you up at the hotel. Just let us know that you have arrived and where you are staying and we will do the rest. Now, Mum, you are to stay as long as you like."

"Well darling, I will be with you for one month and I am looking forward to seeing you both again. So for now I send all my love and I will be in touch again before I leave. All my love. See you soon."

When she replaced the receiver she returned to the lounge where she sat in the armchair and went into deep thought. Within moments tears found their way down her cheeks. Her mind was now going back over the past years of her life. She thought perhaps that after her trip to the United States she should sell up and return to America for good. It was a thought, and just only that, but who knows?

She then got up and walked around the room and looked out of the window to the houses opposite. The neighbours had been a wonderful crowd and so friendly, but perhaps it was time to say goodbye. After all, she was now on her own. She then strolled through the hall and into the dining room which once thronged with the family's voices, but all was quiet now. She then gazed out upon the garden with its well-kept lawn and flowerbeds either side. There stood also a greenhouse where so many happy hours she had spent potting her plants and growing tomatoes. In the far corner of the garden stood a birdbath close to a birdhouse which gave her great delight when feeding the little birds. Her thoughts deepened to the happy days with Phil, but 'life must go on' she thought as she wandered out of the room across the hall and up the stairs to her bedroom. More tears came flooding from her eyes as she gazed upon the photograph of herself and Phil many years ago. How handsome he was and so kind. Yes, he was some hell of a guy. She fell face down upon the bed and sobbed her little heart out. She screamed out his name, "Oh Phil, if only you were here, my dear, it would be so different. But you are not and it's not the same, so forgive me but I think I really must consider living in America with our Phyllis. I hope you understand."

She sobbed herself almost to sleep when the phone rang. It was of course a wrong number but the odd thing was it was a local estate agent trying to contact someone. He apologized for the error but it gave her food for thought. Then she looked again at Phil's photograph and said, "You trying to tell me something, dear."

She then made her way out of the bedroom and downstairs to the kitchen where she made herself a pot of tea and prepared her dinner for the evening. It had started to rain which encouraged her to stay in and remain with her thoughts of what lay ahead in the future of her life.

# CHAPTER 16

The day had arrived for Wendy to fly to the United States. Her journey by taxi to Heathrow Airport was one of many thoughts concerning the past, present and the future. The day had started with sunshine and a blue sky. Perfect flying weather! Upon her arrival at Heathrow she was calm but very nervous and excited. She soon calmed down once inside the terminal and on her way through the departure barrier. The noise of other travellers and the occasional voice of the terminal operator put Wendy at ease.

Soon it was time to sit and relax over a cup of coffee. One thing about an air terminal is you have little time to think about yourself. With her eyes now wandering from one side to the other she noticed that the destination board indicated that her flight was ready for boarding. She made her way to do just that, with thoughts in her mind that in a matter of hours she would be in the United States made her very happy and she once again would be with her family. The journey meant that she would be able to relax, have a meal and see a film, but most of all she could think of happy days ahead.

It was during the flight that she fell asleep, so time was her companion and it went by quickly. In no time at all it was touch down in New York where she had made her mind up to stay overnight at the Astoria Hotel on Broadway. She travelled by taxi from the airport to the hotel and was fascinated by the traffic and the hustle and bustle of its inhabitants. The taxi pulled into the kerb outside the hotel and she hurried inside to make her reservation for one night. Booking in was no problem; she was given a key to her room which pleased her very much. It was cosy and clean and she wasted no time in unpacking and making her way out into the streets where she strolled amongst the New Yorkers. It was the evening that fascinated her as she walked along Broadway where the lights were bright. Taxis were busy, and the noise had to be experienced to be believed. There was so much to be seen and it was not until late evening that she visited a cafe for a light meal before returning to the hotel. She realized what New york was all about. It was not only the American accent that fascinated her, but their confident way of life. They were extremely friendly to her surprise, and very considerate towards her. It was a city with normal people enjoying themselves. She finally made her way back to the hotel and retured to bed. She slept soundly.

As morning arrived she took her time and waited for the family. Upon their arrival and after many kisses they were soon on their way. Phyllis just could not believe that her mum had finally made it and they were a family once again.

It was during the journey that Phyllis said, "Oh Mum, it's great to have you with us."

"It's great to be with you," was Wendy's reply.

"Now Mum, what about you considering coming out here and making your home with us?"

After a long pause, Wendy said, "I have been giving the matter a great deal of thought."

"Well, that settles it. When you return to England you must arrange to sell your house and return to us for ever," was Phyllis's reply.

Where Phyllis lived, it was very colourful, and the people were very friendly. There were many things that Wendy could get involved with and there was so much for her to see. The way of life there was so different to that in England and there were opportunities of so many wonderful holidays to be had in the States.

As the first week passed with happy moments spent with the family it was planned that they would all go and see a rodeo. So during the second week of Wendy's visit much excitement was experienced, for they arrived at the rodeo and took up their places. The day was hot, the sky was blue, and Wendy had never undergone such a gathering of people in all

M

her life. There were the riders dressed in their cowboy outfits as they sat upon their horses in the fenced stocks.

Suddenly the gate was opened. Out rushed the horse with its rider into the arena, leaping and kicking its legs into the air, throwing its mount from one side to the other as he desperately hung on. But alas, after a few moments he was thrown from the saddle. With the crowds now cheering, even Wendy felt part of the atmosphere.

It was during these events that John spotted their friend who was so kind to him and Phyllis when they first arrived in the United States.

John turned towards Wendy and said "Excuse me but I have to go, but I will be back."

John made his way amongst the crowd towards the gentleman, "Hello, Bob" shouted John.

Bob turned his head towards John "Hello John, what are you doing here?"

"Well we have Phyllis's mum from England staying with us for a week or so and I wondered if you would come to our house for a meal this week sometime?"

"I would love to, John. What day do you suggest?"

"How about tomorrow?"

Bob answered with a smile on his face, "That's just fine with me."

"Shall we say around seven? You can join us for dinner."

So it was agreed.

John then returned to Phyllis and explained the arrangements he had made with Bob.

"That's fine. I am sure Mum will get along with him very well," said Phyllis.

After the rodeo they motored back to the house. During the journey Phyllis explained to her mum who the gentleman was. He was of course the man who helped them with their finance to buy their house. They met him when they first of all went to the real estate office to find a house, and it was whilst they were talking to a member of the staff that this man came into the office. He had introduced himself only by name and immediately took an interest in discussing their problem of finding a home. In fact he talked about the finance side of the business which was a great help to them because at that stage they had very little money. After spending a long time with them he had to be on his way, so he left them to discuss further details with the young secretary. It was only then that they were told who he was. He owned the company which had many offices in the States. What's more, he is a lawyer by profession and obviously a very wealthy man. His age is around sixty-three and still very good looking. He took an interest in John and Phyllis which they thought was only because they were English.

Nevertheless, after they got settled down in their new home they invited him home and so a friendship had begun. He was not married, and so time was what he had plenty of, for he was a widower.

The evening arrived for Bob's visit. Everybody was so excited. Wendy looked lovely in a smart navy and white suit with accessories to match. With the dinner now set and a ring at the door, John welcomed their visitor who looked very smart indeed. "Come in Bob, please."

They both entered the lounge together.

Phyllis greeted Bob with a kiss, and said, "May I introduce you to my mum." She then looked at Wendy and said, "Mum, this is our dear friend, Bob."

At that moment both Bob and Wendy stared hard at each other. Bob frowned a little and they both looked at each other with curiosity which was plain to be seen on their faces. Then Phyllis finished what she was saying by giving his surname "Wilder".

Bob just could not believe what he was looking at and neither could Wendy.

Then John butted in and said "Do you two know each other?"

At that moment Bob put his arms around Wendy and embraced her like a long lost relative.

"Well, say something," said John.

"Is there something we should know?" said Phyllis, as Bob released his hold of Wendy and just held her hand.

Still looking at Wendy he said "My dears, your mother and I met years ago in England during the war when I was in the American Air Force." He embraced Wendy again then with a glass of wine in all their hands, they sat down and listened to what Bob had to say. As he looked at Wendy with a thoughtful look on his face he explained that whilst on a raid over Essen his plane had been shot down and he baled out as all the crew did. He landed in a wooded area with minor injuries. Upon being captured he was rushed to hospital where he underwent a minor operation. The report received back at base in England was 'shot down believed killed', but in fact he was well looked after and was of course made a prisoner of war.

He had tried very hard to contact Wendy but found it impossible to trace her as Wendy's parents were both dead, and Wendy had of course taken up other residence. However he did return to England in search of her but failed. After all, England was in a bit of a state at the end of the war. Upon his return to the States he settled down and took his degree in law having found out that Wendy's parents were dead, and not being able to trace Wendy he had assumed she died with them. He eventually married but unfortunately his wife had died giving birth to their first child. The baby also died at birth. He explained that he never married again but concentrated on his business, and so it was that when he met John and Phyllis he treated them as family because he also thought how much Phyllis reminded him of Wendy. She not only looked like her, but she had her similar ways, but he never thought for one moment that she could be her daughter and her maiden name was never mentioned. After all, maiden names are seldom mentioned once you get married and you take on another identity. So all was revealed and Wendy also unfolded her life.

As they all sat and listened it was plain to see that it was true love that began way back in those war years and in the nicest possible way it had always remained, but only in heart and memory. It is plain to see when one looks back, how destiny is planned, and there is nothing that one can do about it. You have only to grab hold of everything that comes your way and make the most of it and this is how it was to be with Wendy and Bob in the future.

Both John and Phyllis could not believe their luck that their mum was really coming back to live in the United States.

The rest of the following two weeks was spent with Bob, of course, and the discussions were mainly around him returning to England and helping Wendy to sell up and for them to return to America and to get married.

Looking back on Wendy's life it had not been a bowl of cherries it had had its ups and downs and the only happy times were with her husband Phil, who was a kind man and who gave her Phyllis, who in turn made it possible for her to visit America and find her first love. You see, the moral behind this story is 'Have Faith'.

# CHAPTER 17

Wendy and Bob arrived in England after a very pleasant flight from the States, and it was agreed that Bob should stay in Wendy's house rather than booking into an hotel. That evening they dined out in the local restaurant and it was during the meal that Bob decided to propose to Wendy.

At the right moment Bob said "Look, honey, there is something I must ask of you." So with a long pause and in a quiet voice he said, "Will you do me the honour of marrying me and becoming my wife when we return to the United States?"

Wendy's answer was quick, "Oh Bob, of course I will."

"Well, honey, I suggest that tomorrow you and I go to London and buy you an engagement ring in that jeweller's shop in Regent's Street where I bought our last ring from. Remember?"

Wendy looked around the restaurant then she opened her bag and slowly took from it a tiny box. She then looked at Bob and handed it to him and said "Why go to London?"

Bob took hold of the box and opened it with a smile on his face and a twinkle in his eye. He could see that it contained their original engagement ring bought from the Regent's Street jewellers all those years ago. Wendy had kept it for sentimental reasons, but it could now be used on a permanent basis. It was a ring with a diamond set inside sapphire stones.

Bob looked up at Wendy and said "I don't believe it, honey, what a wonderful thing to have to happen to us after all those years." As Wendy held out her hand across the table Bob said "This is for keeps, honey, and thanks for keeping it all these years."

Wendy's smile said it all as she admired the ring once again and said "Thanks, Bob." She then continued to say "I brought the ring along tonight because I thought you might just propose to me, and if you had not I was going to propose to you."

The evening came to a close with them returning to Wendy's house.

The following day they contacted the local estate agent and he called at Wendy's house to value the property. He suggested a price which was on the low side, but at least he had people who were interested at that price. So Wendy accepted knowing that the money was not important since Bob was very wealthy. It was also suggested that the sale could be handled without her being in England, so it was agreed that through the solicitor and the estate agent the matter would be left in their hands. All that remained was for Wendy and Bob to enjoy their short stay in England and return to the United States.

During the following two weeks they both enjoyed their visits to London and had a chance to experience their past love and happy days. It meant going to restaurants and theatres, and of course the odd stroll through the London parks and down 'memory lane'. The weather was very kind to them; sunshine all the way. Before they left England, Bob suggested a flight to Paris, München and Austria; so having put the house in order they gave the key to the agent and made their preparations for their last look at Europe.

Their flight to Paris was one of happiness which started by taxis from the airport up the Champs-Elysées around the Arc de Triomphe and into the Rue de Bassano where they booked into the Hotel la Belmont. Oh, what joy lay ahead of them as they first stepped out of the hotel and made their way to the Eiffel Tower where they got the lift to the top. It was a wonderful view showing all Paris in its glory.

Wendy grabbed Bob's arm and said "Oh Bob, is this a dream or is it for real?"

"Honey, it's for real."

After taking in all Paris they made their way down where they strolled towards the Arc de Triomphe where they found a small cafe and enjoyed watching the Parisians going about their way. Near the cafe was a flower shop where Bob purchased a few flowers for Wendy.

Gaily they walked the streets of Paris admiring the shops, and the next day they indulged in a visit to the Notre-Dame, a trip on the Seine and not forgetting the Montmartre which is the artist's paradise.

It was Wendy who said, "No doubt about it, Paris is for young lovers."

"Do you mind!" said Bob "I feel very young and I am having a wonderful time."

When they returned to their hotel Wendy remarked that "I have heard a lot about Paris, but it is a lovely city."

They were soon on their way to München. Now there is a city which holds the past where Adolf Hitler started his empire. Upon their arrival the taxi took them to the Hotel Leopold in the Leopold Strasse. This was a charming hotel but it did not have a restaurant for evening meals so their first meal was taken in a delightful restaurant in the Marine Platz not far from the hotel. It was of course crowded, but the food was out of this world. They were soon to discover that München had changed little, if at all, from the 1930s which made it all very exciting. It was as if you had gone back in time. The walk in the English garden was still a delightful park, where one could relax.

It was whilst they sat on a park seat that Bob said "You know, honey, this is one place I never thought I would visit, or would want to visit, but I must say it is a wonderful city. Now, tomorrow, shall we hire a car and motor to Bavaria, Austria?"

"Oh Bob, could we? I would love that."

"Then that is what we will do, honey, so let's to bed and up early."

The following morning they made their way to a Hertz car office where they hired a small Ford Fiesta. Their journey was simple as they drove out of München and onto the road towards Salzburg and Innsbruch. They took the Salzburg autobahn route, and on their way they had refreshments and then continued their journey to a delightful Tyrol village called Alpach where they would hope to stay the night.

Wendy said, "I wonder what Alpach is like?"

"I have no idea, honey."

Soon they were pulling off the autobahn and onto a road to Brixlegg towards Alpach. A further half an hour gave them the pleasure as they drove up hill into Alpach. The hotel they chose was a wise choice it was called Furstenhoff. It was a family owned hotel where there were extremely nice folk.

Their room was on the first floor and as they both walked out onto the balcony they looked at each other, and Wendy said "Shall we not travel anywhere else, for this I like, Bob. It is so peaceful and its views of the snow-capped mountains and the village below are wonderful. Oh Bob, I do love you."

Several days were spent in this delightful area, but before leaving Austria it was decided to go and see Hitler's Eagle's Nest which is situated in Obersaltzburg. This is close to a village called Rite in Winkle which is on the borders of Germany and Austria.

The visit to Eagle's Nest was one of great excitement because of the interesting journey and of the dangerous Alpine roads leading up the mountain to the one-time Hitler's glory spot. The drive up the mountain is very twisting and hair-raising, but finally they made the first stage, which means you park your car.

Wendy stood and was overwhelmed by the view from such a height. She looked at Bob and said "It's magnificent, Bob, I have never seen such glorious views."

"This is nothing yet, as we now get on a jeep and travel up," said Bob.

The idea of travelling by such transport is because other vehicles cannot pass each other from this point onwards and so communications are established by officials. A further hair-raising view was experienced but that was not all.

When they arrived at the next station, they left the jeep and walked through a vast tunnel which is well lit with wall lights. When they arrived at the end a very large lift awaited them which was the largest lift both Wendy and Bob had ever seen.

"Good gracious! This is some hell of a lift," said Bob.

It was well lit and all the walls had mirrors. The seating arrangement was in green leather upholstery and the lights gave a gold effect. It was very elaborate.

In no time at all the lift was on its way up through the mountain and arrived at the very peak of the mountain. They were, of course, in Adolf Hitler's private quarters which also contained a large conference room which had a stone fireplace shipped from Italy which was extremely large. The view from every window was breathtaking. They both walked around the place and then went outside.

Bob said, "If we thought the views coming up here were great the views from where we are now standing are marvellous. What do you think, Wendy?"

"I'm shattered," said Wendy.

There was little if any wind at all which was surprising, and the sky was blue and free of clouds, The walk around the premises was rather rocky but safe, of course, and there below they looked down on Berchtesgaden and Obersaltzburg.

Wendy looked at Bob and put her arm into his and said "Oh Bob, it's frightening to be up here. It's unbelievable. The views are out of this world."

## CHAPTER 18

After their extensive European tour they flew back to Gatwick and returned to Wendy's house in Surrey. The week that followed was occupied by walking down 'memory lane' and preparing themselves for returning to the United States and putting the final ring on Wendy's finger to tie up the marriage contract. Personal belongings were packed up and arrangements were made with a removal company to transport the items to the States. One more last visit to the estate agent and the solicitor, completed the selling of the property. Wendy need never return to England again.

At that point in time Wendy said to Bob "When I look back, you were my first love and look what I had to go through in order to get you back. Why couldn't I have been just a GI bride as so many were all those years ago?"

She put her arms around Bob's firm shoulders, she looked into his eyes then screwed up her nose.

Just as he kissed her, his reply was, "I understand honey, but looking back that's what makes it all worth while and now we can share a happy ending to our lives." He held her tightly and kissed her passionately.

The next day they made their way to Heathrow Airport. Once inside the terminal their future together began to fall into place.

Then whilst drinking a cup of coffee in the departure lounge Wendy said, "Thanks, Bob, for showing me the continent. It's been a dream that has come true."

His answer was simple, "Honey, 'you ain't seen nothing yet', as Al Jolson would say."

As they strolled through the departure gate towards their awaiting plane they both paused and looked back, they then looked at each other. Bob gave her a wink and she shed a small tear as she pulled her lips together. She sobbed internally and with a sigh she held Bob's arm. In fact her legs almost gave way for she knew that she would be leaving England, her birthplace, forever. The walk to the plane was in silence. They were greeted as they entered, by a charming air stewardess and were shown to their seats. It was of course a jumbo jet and soon they were airborne and there was no time at all for Wendy to look down and see the landscape for the last time. High above the clouds and surrounded by blue sky the meal was the next attraction, and it was not long before they were talking together as though they had never been apart. The smiles from the aircrew, soft background music, and of course, a film show should you wish it; but the two of them were soon fast asleep. Let's face it, they had been rather busy these past few weeks.

As the hours went by, they finally awoke and looked at each other. Bob looked at his watch and said, "Well honey, two hours' time we shall be in the United States when a whole new life will begin."

Wendy smiled and said with great confidence, "Yes, and I am going to live every minute to the full and I just know I am going to be so happy. I am looking forward to it Bob, so very much."

"Well honey, as soon as possible we will get married. But where shall we spend our honeymoon?"

With much thought Wendy said, "You choose. It's your country, darling."

"OK then, how about California, Hollywood, Santa Barbara and many other places?"

"Suits me," said Wendy.

As their plane touched down they were soon safely back in Philadelphia with Bob in his house and Wendy with her daughter. Things were soon back to normal, except for the excitement of preparing the wedding which was to take place in the small local church. Like all weddings there is a great deal to do, but the end product is the same; to unite two persons to share their life together. And so it was on a warm sunny day in July that Wendy finally married her first and true love, Bob Wilder.

## CHAPTER 19

With Wendy now settled in the USA, she often thinks about her childhood friend Denise Povey and wonders what became of her. It was while she was comfortably seated in the garden of her luxury home in California and drinking a cool drink under the shade of a sun umbrella situated on the edge of the large swimming pool, that she looked at Bob as he came out of the pool and said, "I wonder what became of my friend, Denise Povey?"

Bob sat beside her drying himself with a towel, he then said "Why don't you try and contact her, and see if it is possible for her to visit us?"

"That's a good idea. Would you mind?"

With a pleasant smile on his face he said, "Of course not, I think it's a great idea."

She went on to say, "You know, Bob, she was so beautiful, and she became a chorus girl. It would be nice to meet her again. She had such a wonderful nature, she would not have hurt a fly. I just hope nothing has happened to her." She then relaxed in the chair and started to think how to go about contacting her.

The following few days Wendy put a letter together and sent it to her address in Blackpool, but unfortunately the Povey family did not live there any more, and so the letter was returned to the post office marked 'not known at this address'. This distressed Wendy, and of course she was very disappointed and wondered what else she could do.

In the meanwhile, strangely enough, Denise had the same

169

idea, she also said to Glen "I wonder what became of my childhood friend Wendy Dalter?"

"Well the only way to find out is write to her if you have still got her address."

Denise sat down that evening and wrote her a letter and sent it to her address in Croydon, but of course, she did not live there any more.

As the next few days passed Bob said, "Why don't you write once more to Denise? Who knows, someone may pick the letter up, who knows where she is?"

Poor Wendy was so sad to think that she was unable to locate her old friend. Then she said to Bob, "Oh what is the good? Perhaps she is dead?" But for all that, she said "I will write once more."

As usual, it was returned to the post office marked 'not known at this address'.

When all seemed lost, fate played an important part. A young lady who was a cousin of Denise's worked in the sorting office and she noticed the letter marked 'unknown'. She took possession of the letter and when she got home that day she phoned Denise and said, "Denise, I have a letter from the United States addressed to you at your old home. If you like I will post it to you."

"No, don't do that. I will come to you this weekend if that is OK?"

"Yes, of course, I look forward to seeing you."

The days could not go by quickly enough for Denise as she was curious to know who the letter was from.

The weekend arrived, and Denise drove to her cousin's house, which was about thirty miles away. Upon arrival she walked up the garden path wondering who it was in the States that had written to her.

As she entered the house her cousin said, "Do you want a cup of tea?"

"Yes, please."

"Sit down, Denise, and I will get the letter. It's not from a long-lost boyfriend, is it?" and she laughed as she said it.

"I doubt that," said Denise. Her cousin re-entered the room and said "Here is the letter, and tea is coming up."

Denise opened the letter and to her surprise she screamed

out, "I don't believe it. Guess what?"

Her cousin rushed back into the room: "What's that all about?"

"Well, I have been trying to contact my old childhood school friend for some time and it looks as though she also has been trying to find me. Oh, I am so pleased that you work in the post office sorting department. You have done me one big favour, dear." She then went on to explain all about Wendy. Then she said, "I must telephone her tonight when I get home."

The cousin then said, "Why wait until you get home? Phone from here now."

"Oh, I could not do that! Think of the expense."

"Look Denise, the money is nothing after all that you have done for me, and it's family — so do what you have to do now."

"Do you mind. You really are a sweety."

Denise grabbed the phone, and looked carefully at the California telephone number. She contacted the operator who said, "What number do you want?"

Denise gave her the number and she was then told to replace her phone as she will contact her when she has the number.

It was not too long before the phone rang and Denise picked it up. The operator said, "Your call to America is on the line, madam."

The voice the other end said "Hello, who is it?"

Denise then said, "It's Denise. Is that you, Wendy?"

"Oh yes, Denise. I have been trying to contact you."

Then Denise said "I also have been trying to contact you. Now, Wendy, I am using my cousin's phone, so I will phone you this time tomorrow night. Will you be in?"

"Of course I will. Take care, and I look forward to your call tomorrow."

Great excitement was had as Denise and her cousin sat down to a cup of tea. "I'm so pleased that you have managed to contact your old friend, Denise" said her cousin.

Soon after this, Denise was driving home and during the journey she just could not believe her luck to have made contact at last after all those years.

When she arrived home, Glen was there to greet her with a smile.

He said, "Well dear, how did you get on?"

Much to his surprise she told him that she had spoken with Wendy on the phone.

The next day could not go quickly enough for Denise, for she wanted so much to talk to Wendy again. When the time came for her to make her call she anxiously grabbed the phone and asked the operator to make the call. Once again Wendy answered and the two girls were non-stop talking.

It all ended up by Wendy saying, "Denise, will you and Glen try and come to us? We have so much to talk about, and all you have to do is fly here. We will pick you up at the airport and you can stay as long as you like. Please, let us pay your flight ticket."

Denise then said, "No, we will see to it, and we will make a date to come to you soon. This I promise."

The two girls then said their goodbyes.

To conclude this story — Denise and Glen did fly to the United States and a great re-union took place. Much happiness was enjoyed by all, and an everlasting friendship was secured.

It was, of course, only a matter of time before Denise and Glen decided to sell up in England and settle down in America. The money they made through selling Denise's shops made it possible for them to retire and live on a comfortable income. She also provided for her sister Mary not to have to work again. So it was that the two girls who met in 1928 when times were hard (and both went through the war years with stress strain and tragedy but with great determination) survived and lived to tell their stories to each other.